MW01094971

Awkward
STUMBLES
AND FUZZY
MEMORIES

Memoir of a
Peace Corps
Volunteer

By Kathy Ivchenko

Copyright @ 2021 Kathleen Ivchenko

All rights reserved. No portion of this book may be reproduced in any form without permission from the publisher, except as permitted by U.S. copyright law.

For permissions contact: Kathy Ivchenko, kathy.ivchenko@gmail.com

Printed in the United States of America

Awkward Stumbles and Fuzzy Memories: Memoir of a Peace Corps Volunteer by Kathy Ivchenko

Published by Kathy Ivchenko

Ebook ISBN: 978-1-7359042-1-4

Print ISBN: 978-1-7359042-0-7

The stories in this book reflect the author's recollection of events. Some names, locations, and identifying characteristics have been changed to protect the privacy of those depicted. Dialogue has been re-created from memory.

To Curly Boy, Max and Sophia

CONTENTS

CHAPTER 1
THE BEGINNING

Note to self: Never tell your whole family to come to the airport to see you off when you are leaving the country for two years.

Yep, there they are, lined up along the big bank of windows in the gate area, waving. Sisters, parents, and even my baby niece standing shoulder to shoulder, waving with tissues in hand like I am being sent off to war. I am watching from my window seat taxing down the runway. I'm crying too, of course, and wondering, "What the hell I am doing?"

I was headed to Washington, D.C. then on to a country half-way around the world. I knew where the country was on a map, but little else. I'd never even taken a trip by myself!

"Is it too late to change my mind and get off the plane?"

I tried to focus on the tasks at hand. Change planes, pick up luggage from baggage claim, taxi to the hotel. All the while trying hard to hide my fear and trepidation. I was 24 years old, traveling on my own, and clueless. I counted my cash every five minutes in the taxi from the airport to the hotel, making sure I was going to have enough to pay the driver. Anxiously trying to figure out how much I should tip the driver, all while trying to put on the facade of a seasoned traveler. The mantra "I can do this" running on a continuous loop through my head. Later, I would panic about what the hell I had gotten myself into. I mean, really, what was I thinking? I had no idea what I was doing. Nothing in life, growing up in small-town Wisconsin prepared me for the adventure I was about to embark on.

Getting out and seeing other parts of the world was always part of the dream. Live in a different county, learn a different language. Besides all that, as I later told my first Peace Corps roommate, "I didn't have anything else to do." That little mantra got me through a good part of those two years. Every time the idea of going home came up, I thought "What else have I got to do?"

Now you know my dirty little secret. I wasn't one of those altruistic kids going out to save the world. I had just finished college with no job prospects. My love life was nonexistent, especially with the limited pool of potential candidates in my small town. The one guy I was interested in, well, let's just say he was ambivalent to my presence. So, what's a girl to do? Yep, join the Peace Corps.

My family took it well. If they had thoughts of dropping me at the closest mental health facility, they kept it to themselves. An intervention hadn't been planned that I knew about. I wouldn't have blamed them if they did because really, who willingly goes to some third-world country they have never heard of and live there for two years? In my hometown, the unofficial rules were to get married, raise a family, play softball in the summer, maybe join a bowling league in the winter; that is the way it is supposed to be. Doing anything more than a week's vacation in Northern Wisconsin was just crazy talk. Even my grandmother was convinced I was going to die in the mountains of Africa. Granted, she had just watched the movie *Gorillas in the Mist* and somehow thought the Peace Corps involved observing gorillas in the jungle while fighting off poachers.

When I thought about it, I had never felt like I fit in with the small-town life. Where I lived. Sure, I had a typical suburban 1970's childhood. My house was across the street from the community pool, where I spent all my time taking swim lessons and waiting for the rest period to be over so I could jump off the diving board pretending I was in the Olympics. My friends and I would ride our bikes around town without a care in the world. Our parents never exactly sure where we were; as long as we were home for dinner. Picture perfect summers selling lemonade on the corner and winters spent ice skating in the park across the street. Why would I, or anyone else, want to leave? As I grew older, I began to feel more and more like I didn't fit in. I was the super quiet, overweight girl that had friends but never fit in with the cool kids. Let's face it; I was weird by most American high school standards. Always wanting to have the cool clothes and hair, but never quite getting it right. I never had a boyfriend, which widened the gap and made it impossible to fit in. I was naive, innocent, and wanted to do something crazy but wasn't exactly sure how to do that.

In an effort to live a little more on the wild side, during my last year of college, I took a spring break trip with a guy I barely knew. He was a friend of a friend, older, and went to the same college I did. We headed out for a long weekend in New Orleans. Patrick was a nice guy. Tall, handsome and a shock of thick black hair that you just wanted to run your fingers through. He did all the driving and insisted I read the New Orleans guidebook he had brought. I had barely spoken to Patrick before we left on the trip, so it was a bit like an awkward first date that lasted all weekend and hours and hours in the car. We did have some laughs and a lot of alcohol that weekend. I wonder what the statute of limitations is after puking in one of the most famous bars in the French Quarter? I think they would let me back in, hmm, maybe.

My other foray into the wild life was to hang out with a neighborhood family that I grew up around. They were a family of eight boys. Once a week in the summer, they and a bunch of friends, would play softball and go to the local bar afterward. Their main topic of conversation was the *Green Bay Packers* football team, and yeah, that was about it. They had a way of always including everyone, including me. I think with a family that big, it was just natural to include everyone.

I liked being part of the group, and I had a huge crush on one of the brothers. Ahhh, Jake, how could I not have a crush on Jake? The first time I hung out with the softball gang, he put his arm around my waist and gently pulled me back from a towering backyard bonfire, essentially saving my life because of my proximity to the bonfire and the can of hairspray I had used to cement my mall bangs in place. His gesture was obviously a sign that he was totally in love with me and was just taking his time (about two years and counting) to ask me out. Sandy brown hair and, a big weakness of mine, green eyes. He towered over me, even though I was 5'10. He had his brothers' interest in all things sports and *Green Bay Packers* but also had artistic talent. In my mind, he was a brooding, rebel, creative type. I was indescribably drawn to him despite his general polite indifference progressing to mild interest after a few beers. I think most people have a "Jake" somewhere in their past; that guy, that crush, that friend, the one you can't seem to stay away from.

Failing miserably at getting my crush's attention and having the adventurous life I dreamed of, I decided the answer was the Peace Corps. I filled out the stack of Peace Corps paperwork. Months and months of forms, phone calls to check on my application status, and continuing the process until I was accepted. Finally, I received a big Peace Corps packet in the mail. I was excited and still a little apprehensive. The Peace Corps was pleased to inform me that I had been accepted into the program and would be going to Ukraine.

My first order of business: find out where the heck Ukraine was.

CHAPTER 2

PACKING

In-between the occasional substitute teaching and temp jobs, I gathered items and bought things that I thought I would need. Plans were in motion, and in a few days, I would be boarding a plane to a new adventure, a new life.

As the day of my departure grew closer, I eyed my growing pile of crap, I mean essentials, with a wary eye. I was pulling my hair out and staring at my pile of so-called necessities with a dazed, somewhat delirious look on my face. How do you pack to live for two years in a country that you only recently found out existed? My thoughts were alternating between amazement, "I can't believe I'm doing this!" and terror, "What the hell have I gotten myself into?!"

Often, I would ignore my pile of stuff, hoping it would just magically condense to my two-bag limit. Other times, I would silently walk to the pile and give my offering of some new item that just had to be included, then quickly walk away, hoping for a miracle. Other days, in dazed bewilderment, I would walk around my room looking at the growing pile from every angle, trying to convince myself that everything would fit. I refused to put anything in a suitcase in a vain attempt to put off the inevitable. That being the sacrificing of items to leave behind. Finally, the day arrived when I had to put everything in my two pieces of luggage allowed by Peace Corps. Like a tiger eyeing its prey, looking for the weak spot, I went through my pile of "essentials". I added and subtracted at a dizzying pace, stopping every once in a while to check the "recommended things to bring" list sent by the Peace Corps. A deranged, high pitched laughter could be heard coming out of my bedroom. The kind of laugh you hear from the crazy woman that walks down big city streets pushing a shopping cart and talking to herself about aliens.

As the hours passed, I would laugh harder and harder about the recommended packing list. *Swiss army knife*, I would say to myself, "ha, now I can fend off those gorilla poachers- Grandma would be happy." Then my eyes started playing tricks on me as I continued reading the list of recommended items, "mosquito netting?" I would howl, going crazy from the absurdity. Why do I need my triple goose down gigantic winter coat? That was also on the list. It made no sense. Had Peace Corps sent me a packing list for Africa or Ukraine? Apparently, summers in Ukraine are hot, humid, and flying-insect-infested. Finally, with a lot of tugging, pulling, and more than a few choice cuss words, my bags were packed. Trying not to look at the huge pile of things I couldn't fit, I tried to convince myself that I had everything I needed for two years, but even I wasn't that delusional.

I slept a lot on the plane to DC; exhausted from the emotional goodbye and the uneasiness of an unknown future. I switched planes in Detroit, I think. It was all a daze. Landing in Washington, D.C., I had a new struggle. Picking up my bags. My two enormous 50-pound bags, exactly the weight limit, were easily identifiable with their fluorescent-colored handles and zippers rotating on the conveyor belt. The problem was getting them from baggage claim to the taxi. I tried to pile one on top of the other, but it was too heavy for the metal luggage cart that I had bought just for this purpose. Determined to do this on my own, I put the strap of my purple carry-on bag over my shoulder and took one giant black rolling duffle bag in each hand. I made my way to the taxi stand like I was wading through ten-foot snowdrifts. The chaos of the taxi area was a little overwhelming. The taxi counter people must have seen the deer-in-the-headlight look in my eyes and directed me to the next available taxi. It was a bright, sunny day in

DC and that's about all I saw. I didn't notice any of the sights as my taxi navigated the traffic and dropped me at my hotel in Georgetown.

I checked into the hotel and went to my room. I was sharing a room with another soon-to-be Peace Corps volunteer. Her stuff was already in our room, but I would meet her later. I went down to the hotel lobby at the time indicated on the schedule and checked in at the Peace Corps table. More papers, schedules, and a blur of new faces and names to try to remember. Turns out there are three "Kathys" in the group- actually, Kathy (me), Kathie, and Kathleen. It was the fifth grade all over again. That's when my class contained four Kathys, and every time a teacher would call on "Kathy," a chorus of voices rose, singing "Which one?"

My hotel roommate was a short, round-faced girl named Opal with a thick southern accent. Later, when we were in our room, she would say that she felt like this whole thing was "a big ol' hoax." I had to agree, although I would have used the word surreal. In just a few hours, I went from my hometown to a big city I'd never been to before, about to go to a foreign country and not return for two years. Everything was new; names, faces and places.

After an afternoon of sitting in various sessions and the Peace Corps folks telling us a blur of information that no one remembered, most of us went to the same restaurant for dinner. One big eclectic group of people, from the just-out-of-college to recent retirees. Mostly single people, but a few married couples. I was still in a semi-dazed state, walking back from the restaurant through the streets of Georgetown, looking in the windows of the expensive clothing stores. Just looking at these stores and restaurants was different than anything at home. I knew that everything was about to be vastly different from what I knew and grew up with, but right now, it was beyond my comprehension just how my life and sense of normalcy was going to change.

The next morning, my hotel roommate and I were up early. Something new for me as I was never a morning person. This phenomenon should have a name. The excitement and anticipation before a trip that simultaneously keeps you up the night before, worrying that you will oversleep, and also wakes you up in the morning because of the excitement of a pending trip. Opal and I went out searching for a place to have our "last meal." We found a worn-out breakfast joint, and I ordered pancakes as my last American meal. On the way back to our hotel, we stopped at the grocery store. My last purchase in the States was a small jar of peanut butter, *Skippy* creamy.

The time of departure came, and I made my way to the hotel lobby with my heavy bags in tow. I was overwhelmed by a sea of bags. I couldn't believe it—more bags than I have seen in one place. The biggest bags I have ever seen. Bags of every size, shape, and color. Bags so big that it took two people to carry. *What is this? Am I the only one that cared about the luggage limit? What kind of hell is this?* A BIKE, fishing poles! I had a queasy feeling in my stomach, and all I wanted to do was go home and repack. I would have sat down, but I was afraid of getting trampled by the wave of people and luggage going past me. Everyone was grabbing a bag and carrying it out to the waiting buses. It didn't matter whose bag it was. I let the state of organized chaos carry me to the bus, and I sat down, dazed by the experience. A stunned silence overcame me and everyone else on the bus as we rode to the airport.

We probably changed planes somewhere, but the memory is cloudy. I sat next to Opal, my hotel roommate, in the middle seat next to a young guy that fell asleep almost immediately after takeoff. We had to wake him up whenever we wanted to get out of our seats. A couple of people from our group spent a lot of time at the pub table next to the stewardess station. At least that wasn't much different than home. The consumption of alcohol was a part of life in my hometown, as much a part of my upbringing as cheese curds and brats. I was glad to see "my people" or, should I say, my soon-to-be best friends. As we all know, one of the best ways to make friends is to get drunk with them.

However appealing free alcohol is on an international flight, I had no interest in getting drunk in an enclosed space and having to sit upright in my middle seat. I could have easily been enticed to join the group if my seatmates had been more amenable. Especially when I noticed the nice guy, from our group, that had gone out of his way to pull a chair out of my way at the restaurant the night before, had joined the drinking party on the plane. Alas, seatmate fate was not on my side for the long flight. Luckily, the forces of nature came together when assigning neighbors at the training site hotel we would be living in for the next three months.

CHAPTER 3
LANGUAGE TRAINING

We arrived in Kiev, Ukraine, on a cold, grey, cloudy day. Somehow, I thought it was appropriate for a former Soviet country to be gloomy and rainy. It wasn't just the weather. As we loaded on the buses at the airport and headed to our hotel, I noted everything was grey. The buildings, billboards, roads, sidewalks, people, everything was grey. Even the bastion of American influence and commercialism, a *Coca-Cola* billboard at the airport, had a grey hue to it.

I knew next to nothing about Ukraine. I barely knew it was a country. No historical, political, economic, or cultural information whatsoever. The internet was something that I hadn't heard of yet, and I was buried deep in the cocoon of life in Wisconsin. Even in college, the rise and fall of the former Soviet Union countries was not part of my curriculum. I had taken the easy route and remained unaware and uneducated. The only thing I did know was that it was part of the Soviet Union and had recently become independent. That was it. Would I have been better equipped to handle living in Ukraine if I had some background knowledge? Debatable.

On the one hand, if I had gained some historical, political insight, I could have spoken more intelligently on the current status of Ukraine. On the other hand, would this information really matter as I tried to figure out why old Ukrainian grandmas carried plastic bags with pictures of half-naked women, everywhere?

It took a while to reach our little hotel, mainly because it was so far away from Kiev, and the airport was about 30 miles from Kiev. The hotel, where we would be living during training, was a four-story building with two wings off the center stairway. All the single volunteer rooms were the same. One room with two twin-sized beds pushed up against opposite walls, a nightstand next to each bed, and a small desk and chair. Big glass windows lined the wall opposite the door. A tall, narrow glass door with a white wood frame led to the balcony. To the right of the entrance door was the bathroom. A combined toilet and shower tiled and painted in a Soviet Union pink color that we would see everywhere in Soviet-era buildings.

My balcony looked out over the front of the hotel, basically a long driveway that went up to the front steps of the lobby. To the left was the two-story building where all our classes and meals would be. A few hundred feet in front of the hotel was a building site. Big construction machines, an unfinished building with materials laying everywhere, enclosed by a tall chain-link fence that surrounded a half-finished apartment building. The whole time we were there, we never saw more than one guy, maybe two, working on the building. Another Soviet Union-style concrete apartment building that would look like the millions of other apartment buildings.

Training started the Monday after our arrival. Peace Corps put a lot of attention into perfecting their training sessions. A lot of money was spent to find the best way to help people adjust to their new country. Before leaving the US, they try to scare you with how difficult training will be. Schedules and lists were piled on early. Similar to the first day of a college class, you are overwhelmed not only with paperwork but also with the requirements. Ukrainian culture, medical information, and classes on how to teach English as a Second Language were all part of the curriculum. The consistent thorn in my side was Ukrainian language training. It was brutal. Four hours a day, every weekday for three months is not an easy thing to do.

It was no surprise that on the second day of the Ukrainian language class, I was already overwhelmed. It was one of those times that you feel like everyone is getting it, except you. In college, I could just drop the class, never having to admit that I didn't have a clue. That wasn't possible here. In this language class, I was stuck, just waiting for someone from the Peace Corps office to show up at the door, point to me, and say, "Ok, Kathy, time to go." As I packed, they would explain that I had slipped through the cracks and was supposed to have been turned down a long time ago in the Peace Corps application process. "Ah, it all makes sense now," I would mumble while stuffing things in my suitcase. That didn't happen. Instead, on the second day, my language teacher, in all sincerity, told me in heavily accented English, "I don't know how you will pass" after I had failed to understand that she wanted me to recite the letter sounds and not just the letters themselves. Humiliated in front of the class, I hung my head for the rest of the class and wondered if I should take home my jar of creamy peanut butter or auction it off to the highest bidder.

Later that same evening, I sat on the windowsill of my balcony, which would later become a regular occurrence. I shared my balcony with "Peevo" Bob. He was given the name "Peevo" Bob early in training (Peevo being the Ukrainian word for beer). I am not sure who gave him that name, but it stuck. Bob was a big, lovable bear of a guy from Philadelphia. People gravitated to his easy-going personality and insightful sense of humor, including me. He had many friends, and I felt lucky to count myself as one of them, if only because we happened to share a balcony. He was always ready for a beer or shot(s) of vodka. In Ukraine, that was an instant friend maker. Bob was with the Business group of volunteers.

My first introduction to Peevo Bob was when we first arrived at the hotel after our long flight to Ukraine. We all had about an hour to change and get ourselves over to the building next door for a welcome dinner. I got dressed and knocked on the door next to mine to ask Kathleen what she was wearing to the dinner. We had a brief discussion about what to wear. As we were both undecided, I walked the other way down the hallway to see what Bob had to add to the conversation. The door to his room was open, so I didn't hesitate to walk right up to his doorway. As the words "Hey, Bob, what are you wear...ing" left my lips, I looked in the room, and there standing with only a towel wrapped around his waist was Bob. Laughing and shading my eyes with my hands from the view of his half-naked body, I decided that I was dressed just fine and that having a room next to Bob was going to be interesting, to say the least.

Even though Peevo Bob had a regular group of business volunteers that he hung out with at the hotel bar in the evenings, Bob and I usually found a little time, most evenings, to hang out on our shared balcony. We would contemplate the building site progress or the strange little structure on the top of our training building. There was a small metal shed built on top of the building that had a light outside the door that led to the roof. The light outside the door would blink on and off at odd intervals. We wondered if that was where they conducted experiments or maybe sent coded messages to KGB leaders.

So, of course, it was Bob that I told about my anxiety and doubts with language class. Peevo Bob lifted a huge burden off my shoulders with his words of wisdom. As we sat on our balcony, on a warm summer evening, he said, "Look, Kathy, Peace Corps has spent a lot of money on you already. They aren't going to send you home." I will always be thankful to Bob for that little nugget of enlightenment. He was right. Even if I didn't learn more than two words of Ukrainian, I wasn't going home. I was there to stay as long as I wanted. Judging from the rumors and exploits of the volunteers from previous groups, I would have to do something really egregious to be sent home.

I went to class the next day with a weight lifted off my shoulders. Also, as luck would have it, the Peace Corps language teachers had rearranged language classes. I was put in a class with people closer to my Ukrainian language learning level. I still studied and made charts of word endings and grammar rules that I taped to my hotel room wall, but from that point on, I was a lot less stressed about training.

CHAPTER 4

TRANSPORTATION, FOOD, AND STRANGE UKRAINIAN MEN

Before training started to ramp up, our group had an organized tour of the city. We were bused around the city, seeing the historical buildings, monuments, and remnants of the Soviet empire. It was another cold, rainy, gray day. I was hoping it wouldn't become the central theme of my time in this former Soviet country. In a group, we trooped around the city, going to the main bazaar, Kreschatik Street, and Independence Square, among other tourist attractions. Not much available to buy in the stores or markets, not that we needed anything. However, our little group became pretty excited when we came across rolls of toilet paper stacked in a neat pyramid on the table of an enterprising Babushka. Following old stereotypes, I eagerly got in line to buy a few toilet paper rolls that had the feel of newsprint paper and were a sandpaper brown color. There were rumors of a toilet paper shortage at the hotel, and old Soviet Union stereotypes die hard.

Our group was the third group of volunteers to be sent to Ukraine. The first group was a small group of small business development volunteers. The next year was a mix of business volunteers and English teacher. We were Group 3 that also included a mix of business and teaching volunteers. Let that sink in a little because it's important. Our group was the third group of volunteers to be sent to Ukraine...ever. Having Americans and people from other countries in Ukraine were an anomaly. The Soviet Union had just broken up five years earlier. Needless to say, foreigners visiting during Communist times were not exactly encouraged. Sending a bunch of Americans into Ukraine to live and work was as crazy as a young, small-town girl leaving Wisconsin, if not even more incomprehensible.

Cold War propaganda pushed an agenda that Peace Corps volunteers were spies sent to infiltrate the great Soviet Empire. Imagine trying to develop a training program for a bunch of eager Americans to demystify the years and years of suspicion and anti-foreigner propaganda. Ok, maybe I am exaggerating, that wasn't one of the core benchmarks of Peace Corps training, but it was something that volunteers would have to deal with as they left training for cities and villages all over Ukraine.

The weekday training started with the distribution of a full schedule of classes for the next three months. I looked over the packed schedule, trying not to get overwhelmed. There weren't any tests, but there was an expectation to participate in all the training sessions and classes. The training was designed to give as much information as possible so that when we were out on our own, we had some skills to cope with living in Ukraine. We, volunteer trainees, dutifully walked over to the building next to the hotel every weekday for a full day of classes. Language classes, Ukrainian culture classes, medical information classes, teaching English language classes with a practice teaching component, and the dreaded host family stay in the middle of the schedule.

Culture classes were a mix of Ukrainian staff lectures and bringing in volunteers from the previous volunteer groups to tell us what it was like living in Ukraine. Superstitions were a big thing. For example, if you give someone an odd number of flowers, that was mainly associated with a funeral. It was bad luck to give an odd number of flowers for a birthday or wedding party. The list of superstitions went on and on and on. Months later, I would ask my students to tell me all the superstitions they could think of. I filled three or four pages of a notebook and could have probably written a dissertation on the subject.

The previous volunteers gave scenarios and shared their frustrations with daily life in Ukraine. These went beyond dealing with the lack of food in stores. For example, the inability of Ukrainians to say "no" to any request or question. Instead, they say 'yes' and then just not doing whatever was a agreed to.

For example, "Hey, I have a bunch of books donated for use by staff and students. Can we set aside a place where everyone can have access to the books?"

Ukrainian staff member: "Of course, that would be great."

The reality was: "Where are all those donated books so students can read or borrow them?"

Ukrainian staff member response- silence.

There were a few medical classes during training to discuss the medical kits everyone got. It was filled with expired prenatal vitamins, bandages, basic medical supplies, and condoms. The prenatal vitamins were to combat vitamin deficiencies, especially in the winter months when vegetables and especially fruits were impossible to find. According to the medical doctor at the time, it was perfectly acceptable to take expired vitamins. Some of us were skeptical, but what are you going to do? Feeling optimistic about the future, I collected more than my share of the free condoms offered. Hey, I was there for two years, so you never know.

A topic for one of the sessions was what to do in an emergency. I think I crossed my fingers for two years that I wouldn't get sick or injured. There was no way I wanted to go to the hospital in Ukraine. I had heard horror stories of dingy, falling apart, ill-equipped facilities where you had to bring not only your sheets but also buy your own syringes and medicine. Plus, don't forget a carton of cigarettes or cash for the doctor fee. All the Peace Corps reading material said that you would be evacuated to the nearest American medical facility in an emergency. The Peace Corps doctor didn't instill much confidence in his willingness to evacuate people to the States or the nearest military base hospital, especially after he expounded on how the medical facilities in Ukraine were just fine and you could easily treat open cuts with tape or glue, no need for stitches. Umm, no thanks.

The English teacher volunteers, myself included, were a mix of different levels of teaching experience. The training for us consisted of lectures on where to get materials for teaching, and they also brought in a group of teenage students to come to the training building so we could practice teaching. They broke the students into groups of fifteen, with four teachers taking turns teaching English language lessons. For me, it was a little uncomfortable to teach with three other teachers watching. I wasn't confident in my teaching skills and didn't want to be judged for it. We got through it and learned from each other; especially how inventive the other volunteers were. One of my fellow teachers used a song from the movie *Rocky Horror Picture Show* to teach a grammar rule. Another one of the teachers wanted to tape a dialogue for the students to listen to, with one of the characters using a thick Southern accent. Since Opal was our resident Southern girl, she was the logical choice for this role. I am not sure if she wasn't available (where else would she be but in the hotel with the rest of us?) or if she just refused to be used for her accent. For some reason, maybe because I happened to have the door to my room open, I was the next choice for the southern accent part. I said I could do a terrible, fake southern accent. The teacher was desperate, so I made my audio theatrical debut. My character's name was Scarlett, and when Opal heard my admittedly pathetic, fake accent rendition, she faked outraged that I would even try this, as we all laughed. This practice teaching experience gave us a window into the future and the reality of teaching with little to no materials. No making copies of handouts, no poster size paper, and sometimes, no textbooks. We were going to need to be resourceful. The backside of cheap wallpaper would be the favorite tool of the trade, as it could be used for poster paper.

My heart sank as the days were crossed off the calendar, having one less day before the three-week host family stay. I know, I know, I know-host family stays are one of the best ways to be immersed in the culture and learn the language- blah, blah, blah. This wasn't just a step out of my comfort zone; this was a giant leap. I already left Wisconsin. What more did they want?

Those three months of training would culminate in a graduation ceremony where we would become official volunteers, not just trainees. After which, we would be thrust out into Ukraine to sink or swim. No pressure.

On the weekends during training, my friends and I ventured into the city on our own. We had heard, through the volunteer grapevine, about a decent Lebanese restaurant. At the time, restaurants, even in downtown Kiev, were limited. Few entrepreneurs had the money or connections to open a business. This limited the choices as far as eating establishments. The Lebanese restaurant was almost hidden in a nondescript building near the University of Kiev. The main part of the building was a dormitory, but an unassuming door next to the main entrance opened up to the restaurant. It was a good-sized place with about 15 tables. The chicken shawarma and hummus was absolutely delicious, but anything would be great after eating in the training site cafeteria all week. Anytime we were in the city, that restaurant was a must stop over the next two years. Just opening the restaurant door produced an impossible-to-suppress sigh of relief. You were almost always guaranteed to see other volunteers and occasionally the snobs from the U.S. Embassy. It was not cheap, but worth the money.

We were given per diem money during training, but there was nothing to spend it on. There were no restaurants near the hotel we were staying in. Going to the one grocery store near the hotel required running across a busy highway, dodging cars, trucks, and buses. It was also a useless endeavor. Nothing useful was on the shelves at this holdover of Soviet life grocery store. No quick snacks, no bags of chips, and no displays of chocolate bars next to the register. It was a useless square building that always had people in it, but I rarely saw people leave with anything. Can you even call it a grocery store if there is nothing on the shelves but a few giant jars of pickled tomatoes and smaller boxes of unidentifiable products?

Trekking into the city was also a hassle. The trip meant an overcrowded bus, an equally crowded subway ride, then walking, always lots of walking. A crumbling infrastructure meant an old, broken transportation system. It was exhausting to make the trip. Don't get me wrong; I have no problem taking public transportation. Some might say it could even be interesting to take the subway in Kiev. Cavernous marble wonders with escalators taking you deep, deep down into the bowels of the earth. It really is a wonder how they dug those subway stations so deep that it takes two very long, very steep escalators to get down to the trains. The white marble and ornate decorations were kept clean and remained beautiful.

That being said, public transportation, especially buses, are avoided whenever possible due to overcrowding. We were literally smashed head to toe against people from the front to the back of the bus and bulging out of the doors. Having your entire body, not just an "Oops, I brushed against your arm," but completely cemented to someone else from head to toe. This may have been ok for slow dancing to Journey's *Open Arms* at the 8th-grade dance, but not on a public bus with strangers. It was awkward and uncomfortable, especially in the heat of summer with sweat dripping down your back. I had an unusual coping mechanism when I found myself in this situation. I started to laugh. Not just a cute little giggle, sheepishly escaping my lips. This was a deep and continuous laugh that no matter what I did, I could not stop. Tears running down my face, stomach muscles aching, and trying to catch my breath, I couldn't look at anyone I was with; otherwise, the laughing would continue.

Training became routine with pretty much the same schedule every weekday. I tried to eat breakfast once. Let's just say it was unappetizing. Some kind of off-white-colored mush. After that, I chose to sleep a few extra minutes in the morning. Language class started the day. Four hours of small group language class with one break at some point in the morning. Lunch was also in the cafeteria. I usually sat down to see what was being offered and left quickly. Lunch always started with a broth soup. I might have a bite of the potato floating in the soup as I was waiting for the main course to be served. Most times, I left as soon as I saw the second dish was set down. Buckwheat, plain shredded cabbage, a pile of shredded carrots with a spoonful of sugar in the middle, day after day, until I could barely enter the cafeteria. Cucumbers and tomatoes were almost always offered. Which was fine at first, but after a while, you just get tired of looking at them. Little did I know that those precious garden items were a staple vegetable in the spring and summer. In the winter, those green and red gems were greatly missed as they disappeared from the marketplaces and dinner plates. I never considered myself a picky eater until that summer in the training site cafeteria. It was the only source of food. There were no other restaurants that were easily accessible. I had no other choice than to go hungry, a lot. I lost weight, which was a new thing for me. On weekends when I didn't feel like fighting the crowds on mass transit to go into the city, I instead spent the weekend in my room sleeping, writing letters, and eating the occasional Snickers candy bar.

A surprise announcement brought a little excitement to training. Vice President Al Gore was making an official visit to Ukraine, and a bus had been reserved to take us to greet the airplane. On the appointed day, we lined up for the bus and headed to the airport. We weren't the only group at the airport. A group of U.S. Embassy people were also there to glimpse the current VP. It was a whole lot of waiting and waiting. I had no opinion of the embassy employees before I went to Ukraine. I have to admit; I had never given them much thought. I knew they existed, but that was about it. Listening to them lament about the poor circumstances they were living under almost made me laugh out loud. One poor Embassy guy was complaining about not being able to find a dry cleaner in Kiev, and the one they did find would clean the clothes and take all the buttons off and give them back in a separate bag with his clean clothes. Oh, the horror and hardship that they had to live under (written with dripping unspoken sarcasm). Try putting your clothes in a bucket of ice-cold water and scrubbing each item by hand, then hanging them up to dry in the middle of winter.

That summer was my first 4th of July away from home. It was one of my favorite holidays, and my hometown always celebrated with a parade, carnival rides, fireworks, and a beer tent. Ah, the beer tent, a rite of passage into the local drinking culture. A midwestern, or maybe just Wisconsin ritual of mass sale and consumption of beer under a tent in a park disguised as a fundraiser. Growing up across the street from this hub of Independence Day festivities made me homesick to be away during this time of year. I kept telling myself "Remember, you wanted an adventure."

I perked up when I heard about a 4th of July gathering that the U.S. Marines were putting together. It was mainly for embassy type people, but somehow, we (Peace Corps volunteers) were invited. I was pretty excited. What better way to get over homesickness then meeting a bunch of Marines? Visions of big, hunky military men just waiting to meet a sweet and innocent Peace Corp volunteer danced through my head. I decided that nothing in my suitcase was the right "look." I borrowed a button-up, short-sleeved shirt from Peevo Bob with the promise that I would wash and return. I put the shirt on over a tank top and tied the ends together in an improvised crop top. I was pretty proud of myself for being innovative with my wardrobe.

Peace Corps provided us with a bus to the party, but we were on our own for the ride home. When we arrived at the party, there were a lot of people milling around playing baseball, chatting, and an impromptu soccer game started. It seemed like most people only mingled in groups with people they already knew. People dressed in their Polo shirts, matching Bermuda shorts and topsiders. It was obvious from the start that we were the dirty, hippy Peace Corps volunteers; the outcast of the party who were generally avoided. It didn't help that in our group were several people from the previous volunteer groups that *could* be classified as dirty hippies. Greasy haired girls with armpit hair and long-haired guys wearing clothes that had not seen a washing machine in a year. Hygiene efforts were a little lax after living a year plus in Ukraine. Despite high expectations, we (volunteers) partied along with our improvised cups made from cutting plastic water bottles in half, then filled with champagne or vodka. Never say Peace Corps volunteers are not resourceful when it comes to drinking. Most of us ended up leaving before dark so we could catch the subway home. The embassy people got into their expensive cars and went back to their beautiful high-rise apartments, never seeing or talking to a native Ukrainian unless it was through the glass window in a well-guarded embassy.

On our way home from the party, I had one of those odd experiences that you don't even realize how bizarre it was until years later. A small group of us took the subway home. For whatever reason, we were not all walking together, just a little spread out, but walking down the same hallways and up the same escalators towards the same destination. Suddenly, this short, thin guy with a thin dark mustache and maybe in his 20s or early 30s appeared next to me on the escalator and started talking to me in English. It was as if he appeared out of nowhere. I politely said hello, but my eyes were scanning the escalator and corridor for my friends. This guy walked next to me down the long walkway towards the bus stop, trying to engage me in conversation. I tried to walk faster and ignore him, but he kept following me. I wasn't scared for my safety but was very uncomfortable and wanted to get away from this strange man. When I made it to the bus stop, I finally lost him in the mass of people waiting for the bus. The peculiar part was several months later, in the same subway station, this weird little man approached me again. The same place, and the same man. Like out of some spy recruitment novel, he spoke to me in English, and I couldn't get away fast enough. It wasn't until many, many years later that I realized that those two seemingly coincidental incidents may not have been a coincidence at all. Was I one of the volunteers picked from the group that was most likely to be recruited into the local intelligence agency? Or was I just a magnet for small, thin Ukrainian men?

CHAPTER 5
COPING MECHANISMS

Three months of training living in a small hotel, basically in the middle of nowhere, with a group of strangers that quickly become your best friends, wasn't perfect. There were only about 40 of us. Everyone knew everyone else's business. Who was sleeping with whom? Who didn't like whom? Who was thinking of going home? Everyone dealt with the emotional and physical hardship of living in a foreign country and also in a small isolated hotel differently. Some drank more, some hooked up with other volunteers, and some used their womanizing skills to lure young women, less than half their age, back to their hotel room. Well, maybe that last one was something they already did back in the States. But, when a 19-year-old girl in heels and a tiny skirt walked to the hotel with the 50+ year old volunteer with a porn star mustache and Hawaiian shirt unbuttoned down to his chest hair, the rest of the women threw up in their mouths a little bit. Needless to say, homesickness, boredom, and stress added to and intensified the situation.

When the petite Montessori trained teacher and the Citadel dropout both coincidentally missed a Ukrainian culture training class at the same time, everyone knew what was up. I was in the minority as someone who liked this communal living. For one of the few times in my life, I felt like I belonged. I had a group of friends, and although it was hard with bad food, cold showers, and the headaches caused by hours of language class, we all had something in common. I felt I had found what I was supposed to be doing. Don't get me wrong; I had my bad days. Days when I wanted to go home, but I had some fun, too. My room was down the hall from the phone and fax room. This was a common room used by all, because besides a phone, it included a small refrigerator and it was where the Peace Corps Doctor left boxes of condoms (possibly the main draw to the room) and various medical supplies.

I left the door to my room open all the time, and people would wander in, especially towards the end of training when I got a package of candy bars from my Dad. The arrival of packages and letters was a big deal during training. Mail was usually handed out in the cafeteria at lunch time. Everyone would cheer when someone received a package from home. One day it was my turn. A shoebox filled with candy bars. Thanks Dad. Suddenly I had a roomful of new best friends.

Sometimes a small group of us had planned chat sessions, what we later named "Hen parties." I would always offer my room as the meeting location, and people would bring whatever food they had to share. We would sit around and drink, complain, joke, or tell stories. U.S. Regional differences were compared and joked about. Most of the group that came to these hen parties were teachers. A story was shared of a rural school principal that made students with behavior issues pick peas at a nearby field on Saturdays as their detention. Another school that still used "the paddle" as a form of discipline. Both schools were in the southern United States, by the way.

It could easily be said that Peevo Bob was part of my coping mechanism. He was indeed an enigma to me. I liked having a friend to chat with on our shared balcony, and I was also interested in more than friendship. Given my past history of one-sided crushes, there was no way I was going to say anything to Bob unless I was 100% sure that he liked me. From this point to the end of training marked the looking for signs or hints that he might like me, too. A prime example, the time most of the group went to the ballet in the center of the city. Did he keep looking over at me, or was he looking at something else? Was that something? Or was it my imagination? It was a confusing hunt for clues, sometimes we had nice chats, and sometimes he would break off to go meet other friends. As with every other crush in my past, the question remained, "Was he just tolerating me, did he like me, or was I just really bad at picking up on cues?" And don't start thinking I am just making up little hints, that Peevo Bob liked me. During the first few days of training, when we were on a group sightseeing trip around the city, we all had lunch at a restaurant along the way. We had to sit at separate tables at the restaurant because of the size of our group. Almost immediately after sitting down at the table, my table-mates said that Peevo Bob liked me and had been obviously watching me. This without prompting, asking, or generally saying anything about Peevo Bob to any of my new friends.

A few weeks into training, Kathleen, in the room next to mine, and part of my main circle of friends, turned 30. A surprise party was planned for her in the main lobby. Plans were made, and supplies procured. We were all pretty excited to have a diversion, something to celebrate. At the allotted time, we gathered in the lobby area and shouted "Happy Birthday". Music was playing, and the cheap champagne was flowing. It was great to blow off a little steam and take a break from staring at the Ukrainian language conjugation charts I had taped to my walls. I think the term "Chatty Kathy" was coined for me after I have had a few cocktails. Ok, I may not be the only one that this happens to, but it is an accurate term for me when alcohol is involved. I just say whatever comes into my head without censorship and flirt with whoever is in my line of blurry vision. I sat on the floor next to Peevo Bob, who was sitting in a chair. At the end of the night, I held myself up by leaning against his leg and chatting up a storm with those around us. I also asked Peevo Bob to make sure I made it "home" since he was heading the same way. Arms linked (another signature move when I am drunk and liked someone), we stumbled down the hallway towards our respective rooms, promising to meet on our shared balcony. I never made it to the balcony; my bed got in the way.

We had one other organized party that summer because people were getting ornery with the drudgery of training classes. This second party was dubbed the "Bad Attitude Party." At this point, the trainees were getting restless with the isolation of our little hotel and our forced host family stays. It was the middle of training, and the thrill was gone from this little adventure. Language class was dragging on, and a few people had already moved on from their hook-ups. What better way to improve morale than to have a party? Signs were made and party plans were informally organized. We even honored the girl that was supposed to be part of our group but didn't get on the airplane back in June. Rumor had it that this girl had been sent a ticket (yes, way back in the dark ages when people had to have a printed-out ticket before heading to the airport), but her boyfriend proposed just before she was about to leave. The rumor was even exaggerated that the boyfriend proposed at the airport. I am not sure why all of us not only remembered the name of the woman but also the story of why she wasn't in Ukraine with us. Maybe this woman was a reminder of the choice we all had made to leave our lives in the U.S. behind and do something completely different. The theme of the party may have been alcohol and camaraderie, but for me, at least, it bolstered my strength to carry on. I had chosen a different road to go down, and despite the hardships, I had a feeling that this was the path I was supposed to be on.

Our major complaint during that training summer was the lack of hot water. I'm not talking about lukewarm or even tepid water. I am talking about limb numbing cold. So cold it forces you to develop strategies to deal with it. There are three main strategies that people develop to deal with cold water showers. Oddly enough, it was a topic of discussion once or twice, along with the rumors that we would get hot water at some point.

1. The first strategy is for the person that has a strong sense of hygiene. For whatever reason, they feel compelled to go to great lengths to have some sense of cleanliness. This person will get up at 5:00 a.m. and have the morning perfectly planned out. They have a regime of heating water in the Peace Corps issued water distillers. These masochists would heat enough to fill a bucket and take a bucket bath. It takes a lot of time and preparation because the water distillers only produce about two gallons of

hot water at a time. I was a late morning sleeper, so this wasn't going to work for me.

2. The second strategy is the jump in and out method. This is accomplished by putting one part of your body under the cold shower at a time. For the person short on time, this was the best option. To do this properly, one must put one part of the body under the water, get it wet, then take it out and soap up outside the water. Therefore, trying not to stand under the cold water continuously. This technique is repeated until all body parts are washed. Now, the tricky part is washing your hair. I had long hair, down to the middle of my back (hence the nickname "Kathy long hair" among the group and to differentiate between the three Kathys), so this is no easy feat. Here again, you have two options: you can stick your head under the cold water until it is wet, step out, and add shampoo. The other option is to fill a bucket with water and stick your head in it. Both options have their merits. It comes down to how comfortable you are kneeling on the floor and sticking your head in a bucket or standing under a cold shower.

3. This last option takes a lot of stamina. It is not for the faint of heart. I call this strategy the scream and holler. With this, you summon all your courage and pretend you are taking a normal shower. You just get right in and start taking a shower. The inevitable yells and screams of torture are soon to follow.

We didn't get hot water until the last two days of training.

In Ukraine, I had two obsessions for two years. Not sure why. Probably because it was something familiar, a small reminder of home. The first was Snickers candy bars. In the beginning, I ate them because I didn't like the food that was served in the cafeteria. Later, Snickers was something quick that didn't require cooking.

The second obsession was *Planters* cheese balls and cheese curls. The biggest dilemma was whether to get cheese balls or cheese curls. Cheese curls are the obvious better buy for your dollar because there are more curls in a can. They also last longer. However, cheese balls have that wonderful unique texture. There is nothing like placing a fresh cheese ball in your mouth, closing it, and gently sucking the puffiness out of it until you have a small mound of soft fake cheese flavor.

Those lovely spheres of orange and yellow goodness. I had never given those orbs of cheesiness much thought before. Sure, I might pop a few into my mouth when I came across them at a social event, but I never had a truly deep and intimate relationship with cheese balls until I went to Ukraine. There was nothing like the smell of a freshly opened can. Ahhh. What was it about the smell of a freshly opened can? It wasn't like they smelled like cheese or even had a real cheese flavor. I wasn't obsessed with cheeseballs as a child, so it wasn't nostalgic appreciation. However, in Ukraine, they called to me, like a siren song. They were my spirit animal, my obsession, and what I clung to in hard times, which was pretty much all the time. I knew all the hot spots to buy them in Kiev (ok, there was just one place to buy them) and would stock up until a small pyramid of empty canisters grew to rival that of the seven wonders of the world.

I could only find my beloved cheese curls at one store in all of Kiev (the capital city). When I first saw them, I had to rub my eyes to make sure I wasn't hallucinating. I nearly fell to my knees and thanked the snack gods. I don't know how these cheesy snacks got to Ukraine, but oh was I happy when I had them. I usually bought at least one can. Ok, if I am being honest, it was always more than one can (for $2.00 each) every time I went into the city. During training, these snacks were a welcome sight. I would even go so far as to say these little golden nuggets were my saving grace. I would always have some available in my room for late-night hen party sessions or just when anyone wandered into my room. Even after the pieces of orangish heaven were gone, I kept the empty can. I didn't have a use for them, but my little collection grew into a nice pyramid and later made a festive holiday display. I know what you are thinking. Why does she go on and on about cold-water showers and cheese balls? I can't think of a good explanation myself, but I am sure they have some deep and important meaning.

CHAPTER 6

HOST FAMILIES: NECESSARY OR JUST FORCED AWKWARDNESS?

L iving with a host family is something I dreaded even before I left the States. It was a required part of training. The whole concept of a "host family" was something that I never understood the benefit of. Some strange family invites a total stranger to live with them for a period of time. It forces you to have a relationship with these people. What reasons could somebody possibly have for doing this?

I had read quotes from other volunteers all over the Peace Corps marketing materials:

"My host family became my second family."

"I couldn't have made it through my time in the Peace Corps without my host family."

or,

"I lived with a host family for two years, and it was the best experience ever."

I am paraphrasing, of course, but yeah, the whole idea of living with a strange family wasn't for me. I wanted my own space. I wanted to do what I wanted, when I wanted, without plastering a fake smile on my face and nodding to whatever they wanted. I pictured coming home from a hard day and not being able to relax in my own "home" because you always had to keep in mind what was culturally polite. Unfortunately, I didn't have a choice. Peace Corps required a three-week stay with a host family as part of training in Ukraine at the time. Luckily, this requirement was only during the week because that was more than enough for me.

I met my host family in the cafeteria, along with the other volunteers and their host families. Almost immediately after meeting my host family, we started walking to their apartment. It was a quiet walk and, thankfully, not too far away from the hotel. I was distracted during the walk looking for landmarks and paying close attention to where we were going. I tried to take note of every turn and memorize buildings because I would have to do this on my own the next day. If I could tell my host family to "Shut up and don't talk to me, I'm concentrating" in Ukrainian, I would have. My usual way of finding my way around new locations by noting where the *McDonald*'s was located or if the turn I need to take is after the cemetery or next to the blue house was not going to help me in this situation. My host family's apartment building was the same as every other apartment building in Ukraine and all former Soviet Union era housing projects. Towering cement buildings with the same design, color, and building material. Doors, windows, balconies- all exactly alike. No identifying marks or even numbers of any kind. No street signs, and even if the street did have a name, most likely, the next cluster of buildings would have the same street names. Not only were these identical buildings clustered together in a maze of confusion, but every city in Ukraine (and all former soviet countries) had these same clusters of austere Soviet architecture. Going to my host family, I had to be very careful and watch where I was going, or I could easily end up wandering the neighborhood for hours searching for my building or knocking on the wrong door in the wrong building. All of these buildings had the same tiny, closet-size elevators that rattled and shook the entire ride. If you weren't religious before stepping on one of these contraptions, God was found pretty quickly as the doors closed, and the first jolt knocks you off balance. The smell inside these tiny moving closets was a combination of animal urine, body odor, and the musty aroma of age and neglect. More often than not, the elevator was broken, which lead to the adventure of taking the stairs—the same smells as the elevator, but the added bonus of no lights in the stairwells. Walking up eight flights of stairs, with no light or windows and a special blend of smells, while also counting the floors as you go because there are no numbers on the doors, takes a special skill. This was a skill I didn't want to develop. Not to mention the talent needed to tackle taking the stairs when you are drunk. Luckily, I never had to face that challenge.

My host family's apartment was typical of the Soviet Union Era. After hanging up my jacket and taking off my shoes just inside the door (the culturally appropriate gesture when entering all Ukrainian homes), we walked down a short hallway connecting the bedrooms, the living room, the one bathroom, and the kitchen. The room I would be sleeping in was the living room/bedroom/dining room. This room had the requisite shelving unit of brown, lacquered wood veneer and glass doors that were in every Soviet Union home, with slight variations in style and configuration. There was a table pushed to the far side of the room and a couch/bed next to the door. I was relieved when I saw that the room had a door; even with a frosted glass window, it was something I could close. The kitchen was directly across from my room. Down the hall, two more bedrooms and the separate toilet room and bathtub room completed the apartment tour. My host family must have been higher up in the Communist party because a three-room apartment for a family with just one child was unheard of during Soviet times. During the Soviet Union era, the size of the apartment you qualified for depended on the number and gender of your children and if you were a member of the Communist party, of course. I knew a family that had two sons, which qualified them for a two-room apartment. They decided to have a third child, hoping for a girl, so they could get a larger apartment. When the third child was a boy, hopes for a bigger apartment were dashed, and all three boys shared one bedroom.

My host family was a perfectly nice, older couple with a son in his early twenties. The welcome dinner took place in the room that I was going to sleep in. My little host family and I gathered at a table loaded with food as I settled in one of the chairs for a long awkward dinner. I used all my language skills in about five minutes, and then the awkward staring at each other across the table began. The son, Dima, knew a little English, so he would try to translate questions from his parents. The father was a short, thin man in his 50s with balding grey hair and a goatee beard. A stoic, academic-looking man, I learned right away that he was an elected official in the local government from the Communist party. I didn't know the Communist party still existed. Learning something new all the time.

After the initial welcome dinner, I never saw the father again. I am sure that the idea of having an American living in his apartment was the wife's idea. My host mother was a reserved, grey-haired woman that in a typical Ukrainian way, doted on me and worried that her cooking wasn't good enough for me. She was also a teacher of Geography. Their son was a younger version of the father. His blond hair was already thinning, and he had the same short, thin stature as his father. Dima was a nice person, but all I wanted was to be left alone or, better yet, go back to the hotel.

I came up with three reasons why a Ukrainian host family would want a Peace Corps volunteer in their home.

1. Money. This is pretty much the biggest factor, in my opinion. Peace Corps doesn't pay a lot (I don't know for sure), but giving host families anything is more than they normally have. People are maybe making $30.00 a month, that is if they get paid at all. Having extra cash (in U.S. Dollars) coming in is a welcome incentive.

2. Prestige. Host families like the prestige of telling their friends that they have an "American" living with them. In a country where Americans were the enemy during the Cold War, actually seeing "an American" is like a celebrity sighting. Having one living in your home was cause for a celebration.

Before I get to my third reason, it's probably a good time for some background info. I started my Peace Corps Training in June 1996. That would have been five years after Ukraine declared independence from the USSR (Union of Soviet Socialist Republics). For those that don't know, during the time of the Soviet Union, foreigners, particularly Americans, were not exactly a common occurrence. People were curious, excited, and wanted to know what foreigners, especially Americans, looked like, what they did, and especially why they were in Ukraine.

3. The third reason for a Ukrainian family to host an American applies mainly to my host family. I have a strong reason to believe that they were hoping to marry me off to their son. Granted, we were about the same age, but that was about the only thing we had in common. Let me explain first. The son was, on a good day, 5'5, 98 pounds in wet clothes and could speak a few words of English. I, on the other hand, was a well-rounded 5'10 and knew how to say nothing in Ukrainian except "beer". You know the important things.

Luckily, one of my friends and fellow volunteer, Sherri, was placed with a host family in the same building as mine. We tried to get our families together as often as we could to avoid the strain of having to deal with our host families alone. It quickly became apparent that the love connection my host family was trying to put together had changed. A joint dinner was put together with both families. After we finished eating, my host brother asked Sherri and I if we wanted to go for a walk outside. Feeling obligated, we agreed. There were some conspiratorial smiles exchanged between my host family and Sherri's family as we walked out the door.

Once outside, we were introduced to Dima's friend, Andre. So, there it was. Not only a match for Dima, as Sherri was a cute, young girl closer in stature to Dima, but also a match for me. Andre was a blond hair, blue-eyed engineering student and about 6 feet tall. He said he could read English well but struggled to speak it. Sherri and I rolled our eyes about our predicament and continued the walk. For the most part, Sherri and I walked separate from the guys and had our own conversation. It was just such a forced situation. What did the host family think was going to happen? I found the walk more interesting than our escorts. We walked through a nearby park. Lots of trees and pathways, but what I found interesting were the small hills that were remnants of trenches dug during the war that was now grown over with grass. We were walking through the history of World War II.

My host family's matchmaking plans were not too hard to figure out. When a good two weeks into the host family stay, my host brother said, "You and Andre make beautiful children." It doesn't take a genius to figure out what was going through my host family's head. In hindsight, maybe I dismissed that idea too quickly. I mean, here was a handsome guy interested in me with absolutely no questions about it. Setting aside the whole he doesn't speak English and is probably just looking for a green card thing. I am naive, but not that naive. How much easier it would have been to go along with the whole idea. Granted, the language barrier was a problem, but what relationship is ever perfect? Right? I wonder if I would have had *Google* translate back then, would it have tipped the scales in Andre's direction? The amount of time and energy I could have saved. Hours spent contemplating every single gesture, conversation, and body language, not to mention gathering opinions from friends, trying to figure out if Peevo Bob liked me, or hometown Jake, too. Here was someone that already liked me—no need for hours of over-analysis and confusion. With Andre, it was a done deal. Alas, my younger twenty-something self was not as enlightened back then. One of the few ideas I dismissed outright without over-analysis.

I went along with the four weeks of awkward dinners. At breakfast and sometimes dinner every day, I would sit alone in the kitchen as my host mother hovered at the stove, watching what I ate and how much. For mothers in Ukraine, not eating enough was the ultimate insult. The food was good, but I was at a point that I just didn't want to eat so much all the time. I was getting tired of Ukrainian food.

Typical food in Ukraine is bland and made of products that could be grown in a garden and stored over the long winter months. So, we are talking about potatoes, carrots, beets, and cabbage. The summer months brought the standard tomatoes and cucumbers plus lovely fruits of all varieties. The only seasoning used in traditional dishes is salt, pepper, dill, and garlic. I think the training site cafeteria brought a new meaning to the word 'bland' with soups and cabbage salads. They were ok at the beginning of training and soon became tasteless and unappetizing.

Getting homemade food or, better yet, homemade food made with the ingredients you liked was the saving grace of living with a host family. Dumplings with meat or potatoes inside, little pancakes, fried potatoes, and best of all, dishes smothered in sour cream or salads made with real mayonnaise. Yummy. Despite some very tasty food, the variety of dishes was limited, which, for me, led to not wanting to eat and a yearning for the food from back home.

A few of my fellow volunteers felt the same way about living with a host family. We were adults forced to live in these uncomfortable situations. Ugh. One day, a couple of my friends and I decided that for just one night, we would not go to our host families. A rebellion of sorts. United in the shared dream of one less night of awkwardness and forced politeness. We put our plan into action early that day by asking our language teachers to call our host families and tell them we weren't going to stay at their apartment that night. The teachers were confused about why we were doing this, and I am sure the host families were as well, but we were free for the night. Our little band of rebels happily walked to the nearest restaurant, and the only one that was within walking distance of the hotel. Running across a major highway, dodging speeding cars wasn't an easy feat, but we made it and sat down to peruse the menu. Looking at a menu was a useless task at restaurants in Ukraine, but this was the first restaurant that we had gone to, and we had no idea the service we were about to experience was the norm all over Ukraine.

Our waitress arrived and asked us what we would like to order, and the charade begins. Any word we managed to decipher on the menu was met with a "Nyet" (no). This back and forth with the waitress continued until we finally realized our mistake and asked what they *did* have. The reality in most Ukrainian restaurants, at the time, was you eat the one dish that they have, not what is arbitrarily listed on the menu. As we finished ordering and congratulated ourselves on getting out of staying at our host families for the night, we glanced around the room, and at another table is the Director of Peace Corps - Ukraine with another staff member. Seriously! The people most likely to follow the rules were caught mid-rule breaking. A quick whispered discussion ensued at our table. We needed to get our shared story straight. Why were we at a restaurant when the training schedule clearly stated this was a night with the host families: We were studying? We were going to our host family after dinner? We were lost? We don't speak English? Oh, and breathe, remember to breathe. Act natural. The Director stopped by our table on his way out of the restaurant. Excuses at the ready, we exchanged pleasantries, and we were relieved that he was oblivious to where we should have been. Whew!

CHAPTER 7
SO, THIS IS WHERE WE ARE GOING TO LIVE

More than half-way through training came the time for our site visit. This was when we went to visit the individual places where we would be living and working for the next two years. The packing process started again. I packed one huge bag with all the things I didn't need during training, so I could leave it at my site. It was a little easier packing this time. My balcony buddy, Peevo Bob, left for his site visit earlier than the rest of us. I left a good luck post-it on his balcony door the night before he left. That night through the semi-thick walls, I heard sounds that Bob was having a late, late-night guest- this contradicted what my friends had told me- which was that Peevo Bob liked me. I wasn't crushed, but definitely disappointed. Once again, I packed my bags, leaving my nonexistent love life behind. Sensing a recurring theme of liking guys that were not interested in me? You betcha!

On the last class day before site visits, everyone was excited about getting their tickets and making plans with the people that were heading in the same direction. Jen, my soon-to-be roommate, and I laughed as we got the two tiny stubs of paper that were our tickets. Our city was close enough that we would be taking the electric train (commuter train). We had no idea what an electric train would be like but thought ourselves lucky to not have to get on an overnight train to get to our site.

When we asked what the electric train was like, we got vague descriptions: "It's a train that people take to go to their summer gardens," yeah, that's helpful". Soon, the big day came, and we were taken to the train station. Misha, the local go-to person for transportation in the Peace Corps office, took us in his car to the train station and walked us down to the electric train platform. We made our way down the concrete stairs, and all we could see was a large mass of people waiting. As we waited for the electric train to arrive, Misha told a random woman we were going to Nizhyn and asked her to help us get off at the right stop. We soon found out that was unnecessary and useless.

All at once, the people on the platform seemed to tense up and move towards the edge of the platform—a synchronized wave of bodies. We then saw and heard the train coming down the track. When the train came to a stop, a mass riot ensued, at least that is what it seemed like to me. People pushed, pulled, and did whatever they could, even crawling through the open train car windows, to get on the train. Jen and I were stunned. Knocked around by the surrounding chaos, our bodies froze for an instant, and we didn't know what to do. Misha sprang into action, grabbed one of our bags, and started running down the platform looking for a train car for us to get in. Once he found a door we could get in, he threw our bags through the train doors and told us to hop on. We followed orders out of shock more than anything else. As soon as we went up the two stairs into the train breezeway, the doors closed, and the train took off. There we were in the breezeway of the train car with all our luggage and didn't know what to do. One look into the train compartment, and it was clear we weren't going to find a place to sit or stand, let alone put our luggage. It was going to be a two-and-a-half-hour trip, and our decision was made for us. We sat down on our bags and settled in for the long, very hot trip. Did I mention that it was a very hot and humid summer day? A long, long trip broken up by stops every 15 minutes or so. Sweat was dripping down my back, and I was miserable. We had to move at almost every stop to let people on and off and inhale the second-hand smoke from the soldiers coming into the breezeway between the train cars to smoke their pungent full-tar, non-filtered cigarettes.

After about an hour, we started getting nervous because we didn't want to miss our stop. I could just picture the headlines, "Peace Corps volunteers lost somewhere in Ukraine." At every stop, Jen would ask if it was Nizhyn. I had been wondering this whole time, when we did get to our stop, how would the person we were supposed to meet know who we were? I was still naive enough to think that I didn't stand out too much in a crowd. All our worries were put to rest soon enough. When the train rolled into the Nizhyn station, there was a mass exodus. After checking with one last person that this was our stop, we got off the train with every- one else. We only had to wait a few minutes until a handsome young man with sunglasses, jeans, and white, faux leather, pointy toe dress shoes came up to us and asked us if we were "the Americans." As if that wasn't already pretty obvious. I wondered if this guy was part of some sort of plan to get us to stay, having a hot guy meet us at the station. Savvy recruitment approach I must say. Overlooking the fact that he was wearing European white, pointy shoes, he kind of looked like the guy from the '80s Norwe- gian pop group, A-ha. The handsome guy told us, in broken English, to wait there; he would find our coordinator. That's when we met "Olek- sander," our coordinator/contact person.

How to describe Oleksander? He was like a come-to-life animated Disney character; bald, short with a round belly, and probably in his late 50s. He had a ton of energy and was very animated when he talked, ges- turing with his hands, asking a lot of questions, and often answering them himself. When our Peace Corps admin person told us about Nizhyn and Oleksander, he chuckled a little and said that Oleksander was quite the character and had asked that Peace Corps send him "two young girls." This only made sense later when we heard rumors about him personally select- ing pretty young girls from the graduating class to teach the first-year

English students. I think he wanted female Peace Corps volunteers, so he could have some control over what they did and where they went.

The work environment in Ukraine was like the United States, circa 1950, a heavily patriarchal society. Men are the breadwinners and providers. Women did the cooking, cleaning, and child-rearing usually while also holding down a low paying, full-time job in a male-dominated work environment. It wasn't unusual for Oleksander to request female volunteers. It was also in line with typical business practices in Ukraine. A business in Ukraine advertising for an assistant by including a requirement for a young, attractive, unmarried woman was not unusual. In fact, it was the norm. Oleksander was the Dean of the English Language Department at the Institute. The faculty was almost entirely female, with Oleksander controlling it all. A few months later, when I took a trip to meet other volunteers over a long holiday weekend, he asked Jen where and why I was going, because "I can't protect her if she leaves." I guess an independent woman willingly traveling alone in the wilds of Ukraine was not the image that Oleksander had in mind when he asked to send two female volunteers to the Institute.

The four of us and our luggage got in a taxi for the short ride from the train station to the dormitory, where we would be staying for a week-long visit and later moving to when training was over. As we left the train station, I looked around at what would be our hometown for the next two years. A few worn-out (probably drunk) men sitting around the train station yard, a couple of old ladies had set up a low table to sell their vegetables, and a couple of stray dogs sleeping in the dirt, completed the picture of a town that oddly felt like Mayberry from the *Andy Griffith* tv show. A distorted version of Mayberry, but Mayberry none the less. It was a relatively small city compared to other cities in Ukraine, which is ironic since I had left a small town back home to go on this great adventure. But, now, was back in a small town.

A little piece of trivia about my "new" hometown: it was once a bustling metropolis with some Greek influence in its history, which could be seen in the old buildings in the city's central market area. It was also the location of an astounding number of mostly Russian Orthodox churches. Most of the churches were just shells when I saw them. It seemed every time I turned a corner in this town, there was another remnant of a church. Nizhyn was, and still is, known throughout Ukraine for making the best pickles. The reputation for pickle making goes back years and years. Nowadays, I am told there is even a pickle statue. Oh, how I wish this ode to pickle had been built when I lived there. I would love to get my picture taken next to a giant pickle. All kidding aside, the pickles *were* pretty darn good.

It only took about 5 minutes to reach the dormitory. We stayed in a suite of four rooms. However, "suite" is a generous term. Jen and I each had our own room, and another room was used for our kitchen. It had a fridge, table, chairs, a narrow table for a counter, and a standalone shelf with glass doors to hold our dishes and food. We shared a separate shower room and toilet room with two bathroom sinks between the two. This was all connected by a small hallway that led to the main entrance door. There was a fourth bedroom that was locked. We were told that a Missionary couple, John and Mary (appropriately Biblical names, don't ya think?), had their things locked in that room. They were currently "spreading the word" in Albania but would be back at some unknown time to get their stuff. We would hear a lot over the next year about John, Mary, and another group of young believers that were at the Institute before us. Over the course of two years, I lost track of how many times I was asked, "Are you a believer?" Apparently, the only reason for an American to be in Ukraine was for missionary work, spreading the word of God. Jen liked to say on Sundays she prayed to "*Sealy* and *Posturepedic*." I prayed to the same gods, so we had an uphill battle persuading the local population that we weren't there to help people find God.

During our site visit, we were tasked with meeting our coordinator and other faculty members, find out about what we would be teaching in the fall, check out our living situation, and generally get to know the

Institute. A week was a long time to visit a place without any real responsibilities. The students and most faculty were gone for the summer.

Our meals for the week were set up at a local restaurant. We would go there three times a day to eat. It was a small cafe just off the main square in town. There were about eight tables in the restaurant, but that wasn't where we ate. No, we had a special, private back room. Straight out of a 1960's spy novel, this room was down a hall, just past the kitchen. We sat at a long table with 10-12 cushioned armchairs around it. The room was frozen from Soviet times. The only thing missing was a hammer and sickle emblem hanging on the wall. The walls were covered in narrow mirrors and brown vinyl over foam cushioning. A glass-like hanging chandelier in the middle of the room, directly over the center of the table, completed the look.

What set this room apart was that it had a hidden door. Once the main entrance door was closed, it blended in with the wall décor and the door was undetectable. If there was another door or perhaps a recording room behind the mirrors, I didn't know. It was the perfect place for secret KGB meetings with leaders in the Communist party. When we were in this room, we made sure to speak loudly and clearly, asking for a washing machine and Doritos, just in case there was a microphone hidden in the chandelier. Couldn't hurt to ask.

On the first day after our train trip, we went on a tour of the Institute. I was stunned to see the main building. A magnificent white-columned building that was huge, old, and amazing. Almost like a palace. We learned that it was built by Catherine the Great's Finance Minister around 1805. Thick walls, towering wood doors, and massive windows. Overgrown trees and neglected gardens surrounded the building. It was not hard to imagine the horse-drawn carriages driving up the circular drive to the front steps of the Institute, dropping off the sons of noblemen pursuing their education. The institute's big claim to fame was that Nikolai Gogol studied there. At the time, my knowledge of Russian literature was almost non-existent, but I had two years to read up on the subject and find out who

Nikolai Gogol was. Now you may be thinking "why isn't she telling me who Nikolai Gogol was?". Well, I could tell you he was a Russian author, born in Ukraine....., but no. Look it up, without the internet, struggle like I did. And no, Nikolai Gogol was not another one of my crushes.

After a day or two in Nizhyn, it was politely suggested to us that we didn't need to stay the whole week. All the students were gone, and the staff was busy with whatever they did in the summer. Our day consisted of walking to the restaurant three times for meals, in-between laying on the bed in our rooms, staring at the walls. After a few sleepless nights of listening to roosters crowing all night and dogs barking all day, we were happy to head back to our training hotel. It was unbelievably hot that day we took the electric train, then the subway, then finally a near-empty bus back to the hotel. Sweat running down my face and soaking my clothes the whole time, I was miserable. For once, I was looking forward to a cold shower back at the hotel. It took most of the day to get back to the hotel. Then still more days of nothing to do until the rest of our group returned from their respective sites.

Peevo Bob and I had a running joke. Peevo Bob was a morning person and usually up early. I was not. We both slept with the doors to our joint balcony open in order to get some fresh air in the rooms. The joke was, on many mornings he would call out "Good morning, Kathy" when he heard the metal springs on my bed squeak, before I had fully woke up, just to tease me. A couple of times, he called out before my bed squeaked, and I hadn't even opened my eyes yet. To this day, I don't know how he managed the timing on that so well. Bob arrived back the day after we did, early in the morning. I heard him in his room and then out on the balcony. I turned over in my bed, exaggerating the squeaking of the bedsprings. Then came the tentative "Kathy?" Laughing, I went out on the balcony. I wanted to run over and give him a big hug. I was so happy he was back. However, remembering the sounds in his room the night before he left for his site visit, I held back. Not even sure what those hopes were for Bob and I, but I knew it wasn't going to happen. Oh, well. There were only a couple of people back that day. We hung out together in one of the lobby areas, chatting and generally wasting the day with a couple of other people that had returned early.

Slowly throughout the next day, people returned from their site visits. A small group of us gathered in front of the hotel sitting on benches and welcoming the late arrivals with offers of champagne and tissues. We shared stories of our adventures- the good, the weird, and the bad. Little did any of us know just how important that site visit was and the effect it would have on the next two years. People told stories of English teachers that didn't speak English, volunteers being taken to a small room in a stranger's apartment and left there the whole time having no contact with anyone, and a volunteer having not been shown where they were going to live or work. Not surprisingly, those volunteers with less than great experiences during their site visit left before the end of their two-year stint. However, we didn't know that at the time.

I don't remember who brought the alcohol out that night, but with all the storytelling, the champagne was flowing freely into our repurposed water bottles and coffee cups. It was a beautiful evening with a slight cool breeze blowing. We all just needed to unload, vent, and laugh. At some point, the champagne ran out. It was one of those defining moments when you are drinking, and the night reaches a turning point. It could turn into a historical event talked about for years or wither away into obscurity. That moment in the night (always late at night) that someone makes the most brilliant suggestion ever, and it changes the very essence of the gathering. In this case, that defining moment was the suggestion to switch to hard liquor.

It was a logical step in the minds of many at that particular moment and time. The champagne had run out, but we remained undaunted and unwilling to call it a night. Someone brought out the vodka. I'm still not sure who brought it out or had the foresight to have a bottle of vodka on hand. None the less, vodka was poured, and the merriment continued.

Carrying on in the true spirit of a Peace Corps volunteer in Ukraine, we finished the vodka, too.

A bit of advice about drinking alcohol in Ukraine. Champagne is cheap and tasty. Vodka is also cheap and a staple in most homes. At any given celebration, of which there are many in Ukraine, both alcoholic beverages could be found on the table. Here is the advice, DON'T MIX THE TWO! Let me be clear; do not start drinking shots of vodka and then switch to sipping champagne, and don't start drinking champagne, then do shots. If you take away nothing from my musings of the past, then I have failed. Learn from my mistakes. This newbie made the champagne sipping, vodka shotting mistake and ended the night on the bathroom floor curled around the toilet, mumbling about the room spinning and praying to whatever god would listen. Somehow, the alcohol gods were not listening to my pleas to end my suffering that night. Nor did it stop me from drinking again.

CHAPTER 8
THE END OF TRAINING AND ADJUSTING ALL OVER AGAIN

The end of training had finally arrived. Surprisingly, to me, anyway, one of the volunteers in our group, Joey, decided to go home. He was the first one in our group to leave. At the time, I didn't reflect on his leaving, but it was significant. I was surprised by his departure because the thought of going home hadn't even occurred to me. It wasn't even considered a possibility in my mind. Maybe I was having fun? Maybe I was curious to see what life would be like at my site? Maybe my life in Wisconsin had already lost its appeal? Who knows? I was staying; that was one thing I was certain about.

Joey's father was having some medical issues, but another contributing factor may have been that this trainee was going to a site with one of the "favorites" in the group. This favorite volunteer had an amazing ability to learn the language, and whom I would describe as an intellectual. Don't get me wrong, a nice person, very intelligent and personable, but I can understand the reluctance to go to the same site as this favorite. Living in the shadow of someone staff would fawn over is not an enviable position to be in. Comparisons would inevitably be made between the two volunteers.

The day after the graduation ceremony, we all said goodbye to the guy leaving early and wished him well.

The day of the trainee-to-volunteer graduation ceremony was finally here. Excitement and enthusiasm for the future were at a peak. Anyway, I don't remember any discussions about how we were feeling about heading out to our individual sites in Ukraine. As a group, we had survived training and bonded. Lifelong friendships had been made. Nothing was going to change the fact that we had all gone through the emotional ups and downs of training together. Even years (many years) later, there is still a connection we feel towards each other as former Peace Corps volunteers in Ukraine, Group #3. You would think this sort of reflection would be saved for the end of my rumination, but that isn't the sort of gal I am. I feel that training was a significant part of my experience. I may have lost touch with some people from my group, especially those that left before the end of their two years of duty, but that doesn't make them less important.

We all got dressed up and headed to the Museum of Medicine for our official "Becoming a Peace Corps Volunteer" ceremony. Until this point we were only trainees. The Medical Museum was a strange choice for a venue, but it had a stage and a small reception/lobby area. We were all so excited, at least I was. Finally finished with training!

After the ceremony, I blasted Aretha Franklin in my room and danced around drinking champagne straight from the bottle, before the reception even started, joined by a few friends. The reception was in the building next to the hotel where all the classes took place. A long table heavy with food and a lot of booze. A river of champagne and vodka flowed, and we danced our asses off. I danced with the sleazy, young girl chaser and was surprised to find him a good dancer. I also slow danced with Peevo Bob and thought about asking if we would ever be more than friends. Fully aware, or as fully aware as a mind can be when soaked in alcohol, that it was way too late in the game to ask questions of this nature. And I probably didn't want to know the answer anyway. After all, we were heading our separate ways, within Ukraine, tomorrow. The crowd started to thin out, and we, or more correctly, I stumbled my way back to the hotel. I was walking with Peevo Bob and, despite my awareness it was way too late in the game, decided that night was a good time for my drunk self to ask him those lingering questions. Was he with that other volunteer? Did he like me? Did he want to be more than friends? Given it was our last night of training and I was totally smashed, obviously I had a well thought out plan. I forged ahead undaunted and followed Bob into his room. The conversation went something like

"Um, Bob, do you have anything you want to say?

"What?"

"Anything you want to say?

"Kathy, what do you want me to say?" as he literally falls into his bed, and I am leaning against the balcony door, trying to keep myself upright.

I leave his room in a huff and pass out in my own bed.

My recollection is fuzzy, but in the end, that is about the extent of the conversation. So much for my alcohol-infused bravado.

The next day was the day of departure. Jen and I were one of the first groups to leave. Most of the other volunteers were either lingering around the lobby or waving goodbye from their balconies. Jen and I put our bags in the Peace Corps car. Peevo Bob had carried one of my bags and followed us down to the lobby to see us off. Despite my awkward and admittedly vague attempts to change our status the night before, Peevo Bob and I were still good friends, signed and sealed, and that is what we would always be. This also finally brought the realization that he wasn't interested in being anything more than friends, and I was ok with that. A big hug and a few waves and Jen and I were heading for the train station. We were taking the regular train this time. The first stop was Nizhyn, and it would only be stopping for a few minutes to unload. Before I knew it, we were dragging our bags into the dormitory and settling into our little suite of rooms. We had arrived at our new home for the next two years, eager to jump right in and save the world.

Then the waiting began. Oleksander, our coordinator, told us that classes wouldn't start for a few days, then a few days more. Pretty soon, we were wondering if they would start at all. We spent endless hours in our rooms. I wrote letters home, took long naps, read, and pretty much screwed up my circadian sleep rhythm. It happened so fast. I was up until really late at night and, of course, sleeping until almost noon. When classes finally started, I kept the same schedule since my classes were all in the afternoon and never started before 1 pm. During training, one of the other volunteers in my group came up with a brilliant quote that I have always remembered. He said, "If you sleep 12 hours a day, you are only here for one year." Bam. Such an applicable and useful phrase. You are welcome.

I was teaching at a Teacher Trainer Institute, which meant my students were in college to become teachers of English and German. I was going to be teaching a reading course. The assigned book was *To Kill a Mockingbird by Harper Lee*, one of my favorites. Over the semester, I would be assigning pages that the students would read and then discuss in class. Those first days of absolutely nothing to do, I had planned out the whole semester with assigned pages, discussion questions, and lesson plans. I had also decided to add different lesson plans and teaching methods, all using *To Kill a Mockingbird* as the subject matter. It was a teacher training institute, after all. Although, if you asked my students, I could probably count on one hand the number of students that wanted to be teachers. They all wanted to be translators and saw dollar signs by becoming an English translator.

The American couple, the biblical John and Mary (yes, those were their names), were at the Institute living and spreading the word of God before Jen and I came. The elderly missionaries had set up to eat their meals in the building next door to the dormitory. Entering the building through a side door and up a back stairway that was next to the kitchen, John and Mary ate lunch and dinner there during the week. Jen and I continued this weekday trek to the cafeteria twice a day. The building used to be the Institute's cafeteria back during Soviet times but was unused now.

They still had employees and a kitchen stocked with equipment, but food, not so much. The ladies that worked in the kitchen were nice and always smiling. Jen and I dutifully walked over twice a day for the first couple of months. At this point, I had lost some weight during training and continued to as we went to the cafeteria every day. Day after day of the same food with little variation put in front of us, and I couldn't take the monotony. Cucumbers and tomatoes to start every meal. I started pushing the dish away as soon as I sat down and waited to see if the second course was going to get any better.

One day, I sat down to a small mound of shredded carrots with a heavy spoonful of sugar sprinkled on top and a few raisins. I was losing it. I couldn't even look at the plate. This might have been a clue to my junk food addiction but moving to Ukraine had made me quit cold turkey. The whole country was a forced rehab facility for junk food addiction. Towards the end of the first semester, the ladies that cooked our meals began to "forget" that we were coming. Either that or they didn't have anything to feed us. When it began happening a couple of times a week, we just stopped going altogether.

A little more background: This period of time was five years after the breakup of the Soviet Union. The economy was terrible, to say the least. The value of the local currency kept dropping lower and lower. We were paid a stipend each month, and luckily, it was in dollars because the local currency was so unstable. We had money to spend, but nothing to spend it on. Food in stores was hard to find. On any given day, a store might have milk on the shelves. The next day, the same store would be out of milk, possibly for weeks or months. The main place to buy products like eggs and meat was the open market or bazaar. Best to ignore the tons of flies and wild dogs swarming around large slabs of meat sitting outside on tables in the hot summer heat and the bitter cold of winter. Eggs were usually a safe purchase unless one slipped through that was left in the chicken coop too long. Don't even think about fresh vegetables and fruit in the colder months. The colder the weather, the more vegetables started to disappear from the stores and the bazaar.

After a while, vendors' faces become familiar, and you develop a habit of buying from the people you recognized, like the pickle lady who had the crunchiest and best-tasting pickles at the bazaar. Every week, she was selling her homemade canned goods in the same spot. If the pickle lady wasn't there, then it was a sad, pickle-less week. The only thing you could count on was the bread in the bread stores. Even that was a hassle. Bread lines out the door were a common sight. I am not kidding; people lined up outside the bread store. Just like the Soviet Union stereotype. Bread line rules needed to be followed and were strictly enforced by those in line. When you join the line, it must be at the end—no cutting in line. The only exception was for little old ladies. Even then, skipping the line depended on how surly the crowd was outside the store. And always remember that at any time, while standing in line, that you will have one or more people come up to you asking if the bread is fresh. Getting to the front of the line and purchasing fresh bread was cause for a celebration. It was hard not to stop at a kiosk on the way home for a bottle of champagne to celebrate a fresh and delicious purchase. I found myself on many occasions standing in those lines hoping they had fresh, warm white bread loaves and often settling for the dark Russian black bread. It was a situation where you took what they had, not what you wanted.

CHAPTER 9
WHY IS EVERYTHING SO HARD?

Classes did eventually start after about two weeks of staring at the walls and writing letters home. Jen and I settled into a routine. English language classes were taught in the afternoon. I taught what was called "Home Reading," a class based on a novel. Other than giving me the book, *To Kill a Mockingbird*, little other direction was given. I assigned a certain number of pages of the book, and it was up to me what I did in class. My students were fourth-year students, and their English was very good. I tried to mix things up with lesson plans for each section of assigned reading materials.

My main goal was to get them talking in English and make sure they read the book. I also put together an American Culture class for the fifth-year students. This class was totally up to me as far as content. Thinking I was very clever, I started the American Culture class comparing the Walt Whitman poem, *I Hear America Singing*, the Langston Hughes poem, *I, Too, Sing America*, and the lyrics from the Billy Joel classic, *Piano Man*. All written out on the back of the wallpaper and hung in the classroom on clothes hangers. If I wasn't carrying my purple bag filled with unusual teaching materials to class every day, something was wrong. We would talk about American stereotypes and a number of other topics that the students came up with. My favorite classes were when I could get my students to laugh. Making observations about everyday life in Ukraine and discussing it with my students was a good way to get them talking or outright laughing.

One day in class, I started making a list of superstitions in Ukraine, of which there are many. I filled four pages of a notebook with examples, such as it was bad luck for a single female guest to sit at the corner of a table for a meal. It means she would not get married. Many of the superstitions were centered on the countless ways women were bad luck. I don't know the origins of how these superstitions came about, but it's fascinating how these women-centered superstitions were used to keep women in their place in a male-dominated society. I also used them to get a laugh out of my students by pointing out their absurdity. For example, the superstition that if you left your house and the first person you met was a man, that was good luck. My students laughed out loud when I described leaving my dorm rooms every day because directly across from my main door was the office of the "Komendant." All the students knew who this heavyset, middle-aged woman was. The Komendant was the head person of the dormitories, ruling with a stereotypical iron fist and a picture of Lenin on the wall next to her desk. She had one arm, and it was easy to imagine her not taking any crap from students as she used her one arm to toss behavior problems out the door of the dormitory. My students found it hilarious that this was the first person I saw most days. I had never said more than "hello" to the Komendant, but when I did speak to her, she had the sweetest smile, despite her intimidating appearance.

My favorite time I got my students to laugh was the first day of the second semester of my second year in Ukraine. I tried to have lesson plans that were different than the rote memorization and standard dialogues from their other classes. I taught these students for almost two years, and they knew my teaching style was a little unorthodox. I couldn't have planned their reaction if I tried. I handed out one blank piece of paper per student at the beginning of class, intending to do a fun ice breaker activity to get the students talking. At the last minute, I announced that with the paper, they were supposed to write a summary of the book from last semester. Thinking I would get a little giggle out of the students; instead, the room got quiet, and they were deep in thought and starting to put pen to paper, working on the summary. Surprised at their reaction, I blurted out, "Wait. I was kidding!" The students burst out laughing so hard tears came to many eyes. When they regained their composure, I asked them, "Did you really think I would make you write a summary of a book from last semester?" The answer was a resounding "yes" because that is exactly what their other teachers would do.

Jen and I were just a few years older than our students. We got along great with them, and they would often visit us in our dorm rooms to practice their English. The faculty, on the other hand, was a little stand-offish. It could have been because of our age or their insecurity about their English, but the other teachers didn't go out of their way to talk to us. There wasn't an opportunity to mingle with the other teachers either—no teacher's lounge or faculty mixer to ease the awkwardness. Most of the time, Jen and I would go teach our classes then head back to our dormitory rooms. I considered myself lucky to be teaching at what was essentially a University. One of my friends/fellow volunteers taught middle school age students at a public school in a big city in Ukraine. The students took advantage of her sweet, naive nature and caused such disruption in her class that she ended up leaving Ukraine early.

Teaching in Ukraine wasn't perfect. At the end of my first year of teaching, a student came up to me in the common area of the English classrooms and said he wanted his grade for my class. I had never seen this student before, yet he expected me to give him a grade. I told the student that I couldn't give him a grade because I didn't know who he was, and if he wanted to take my final exam, he could come to class. In the end, it didn't matter. I calculated grades, took attendance, and gave quizzes and tests, but no one ever asked me for my student grades. Not sure how those students got their final grades for my class. I was never asked about grades. The policy for the Institute was, that all students had at least three tries to pass their classes at the end of the year. The final exams were oral exam questions. A lot of times, the same questions were asked at each try the student took to pass the final. The last attempt to pass the final exam was with the Dean of the English Department. I had heard that at final exam time, it wasn't unheard of for students to show up for the exam with champagne, chocolates, maybe even a cash gift. I told my students as, I was explaining my grading system at the beginning of the semester, that I accept bribes- chocolate, homemade food, etc., just to see their reaction. Got a few laughs with that, but no chocolate at grading time.

Having Jen as a roommate was so helpful. Not only did I have someone to talk, laugh, and complain to, but she forced me to not descend into total laziness. I could have easily coasted through my time in Peace Corps by staying in my room, teaching my classes, and that was it. Not taking the easy way out was a battle for me to overcome. So, when Jen wanted to continue with Ukrainian language lessons, I climbed on board. Peace Corps paid for us to hire a language tutor. Oleksander, our coordinator, choose two young women, that who were English teachers for the first-year students, to be our Ukrainian language tutors. Once a week, they would come to our dorm rooms for a one-hour language lesson. Jen and I each had individual lessons. The tutors were very sweet, and sorry to say, easy to manipulate into speaking more English during the lesson than Ukrainian. Not proud of myself, as I didn't put much effort into studying or learning the language. The lessons continued semi-regularly until the second semester, when they just kind of dwindled down and stopped. Laziness took over, and thoughts of my Ukrainian life being a little easier if I could ask questions and easily buy things, disappeared. I muddled through when out in public. In my classes, I only used English; in fact, I tried to say something in Ukrainian in class one time, and the students just laughed. Not exactly the encouragement I needed to resume my studies.

Everything was an ordeal. Shopping, travel, just everyday life had some kind of obstacle to overcome. Maybe it was going to four different stores to buy butter and then still coming home empty-handed. Or maybe it was being a functional illiterate in society. Or maybe it was having to walk everywhere because the buses were so crowded, people were hanging out the doors. Adjusting to one's circumstances involved asking yourself a thousand times a day, "Why am I putting myself through this constant frustration?"

Jen and I were on our own food-wise on the weekends. We had a one-burner hot plate and two pots. One of our first purchases as roomies was a little oven that could sit on the counter. It had one switch, on/off. No idea what temperature we were cooking at, but it worked pretty well for us. Jen found it one day in the only department store in town. Although, department store is a generous term. It was basically a leftover remnant of the state-owned Soviet Union stores. Store shelves were sparsely lined with random, mostly useless items. Although, one time, I did purchase a Milwaukee Bucks baseball hat with an old logo on it, probably from 1972. Jen and I went halfsies on our cute little "easy bake oven". We were so proud and excited about the purchase. This little purchase would expand our culinary possibilities exponentially.

Ukraine has an ingenious way of dealing with shoplifting in their stores. Everything, and I mean, everything, is on shelves behind glass display counters. The shelves are not lined with stacked boxes of new toasters and blenders. It was more like a bunch of random unboxed stuff sitting on the shelf, an extension cable next to a headscarf next to a tea set wrapped in cellophane was a typical and well-stocked store. A careful perusal of the shelves is required to make sure you don't miss something. This makes touching things before you buy them difficult and forget about trying on clothes before purchasing them; that is impossible. This also can make the customer feel like a complete idiot. It reduced the buyers, or more specifically, me, to a level below functional illiteracy. At least as a functional illiterate, you can speak and communicate with people. In this circumstance, I was reduced to pointing and making low guttural sounds hoping they resembled something that the salesperson would understand, so I could get what I wanted and get out of there. Of course, that was never the case.

After asking to see the product, I must give it back and go to the end of the counter, tell the person the price I need to pay, pay, bring the receipt back to the salesperson who is now gossiping with her co-worker, tell her what I am purchasing (because even if I am the only one in the store, she can't be expected to remember what I looked at a minute ago) and then hopefully get the product I have been hoping to purchase. Now, there are ways around this. I can write the amount on a piece of paper or buy something that costs an amount I can pronounce. The latter does have some drawbacks. Hence, the infamous cheese buying incident of 1994. You haven't heard of it? I'm sure it was a headline in the local Ukrainian newspapers.

This particular incident happened during training. I was sick of the food in the cafeteria and wanted some kind of food or snack that I could have in my room whenever I wanted. I walked from the hotel to a recently found, small, one-story building that was called a grocery store. What little products they had were in deli cases along the interior walls. I looked around, but not much there was of interest. Some sausage, cheese, and things I didn't know what they were. I'm guessing dairy products, but who knows. I settled on some cheese in one of the deli cases. It was a big wheel of some kind of white, possibly hard cheese. Well, I thought maybe I could get some cheese and put it on bread. It didn't occur to me that I didn't know where to buy bread. There wasn't a bread store nearby that I knew of. I have no idea what I was thinking.

Now that I had made my decision, I had to make the purchase. I walked up to the case and quietly asked for cheese, pointing to the big white hunk behind the glass. The woman working behind the counter said something to me, and I could only catch the word for how much. It seemed like a long sentence when just the word for "how much" would have been more than enough. That's when the panic started. I had no idea how to say how much I wanted. I knew that it was sold in kilograms as a unit of measurement but wasn't exactly sure how much that was or even the word for "half" or "just a little bit."

So, with a look of pure helplessness on my face, I told the woman I wanted one kilogram (a little over two pounds) of cheese. If she thought that amount was weird, her stern Soviet facial expression didn't give anything away. Then the woman continued speaking in Russian to me and gesturing towards the center of the store. I was taking a Ukrainian language class, but I doubt that would have mattered if the woman had been speaking Ukrainian. I still wouldn't have known what she was saying. Our language class hadn't covered how to buy things in a store yet. I had no idea that the woman was telling me to pay the cashier sitting in the wooden desk/box in the center of the room, similar to a judge's desk in a courtroom. Confused, I walked in the direction the woman was pointing. As I walked, the woman behind the counter and the cashier yelled to each other. I couldn't translate, but I am pretty sure they were saying, "This idiot foreigner is buying an entire kilogram of cheese. She must be from Wisconsin."

I learned how to cook in the Peace Corps. Well, not me, but I was good at watching my roommate, Jen, whip up some lovely culinary masterpieces with the few food staples we could find at the bazaar. Before Peace Corps, my repertoire consisted of soup from a can or maybe a grilled cheese sandwich. We had so much time on our hands, and with the monotonous food from the dining hall during the week, cooking on the weekends became a much-anticipated event. My step-mother had sent me a copy of her church's cookbook. We would pour over the cookbook like it was a Bible, doggedly searching for recipes that could be made with what we had available. Sadly, we had to eliminate all recipes that included Campbell's condensed soup as an ingredient, a surprising staple food of small-town life, or maybe Wisconsin in general. Jen was the cook in our little family. I would help with the shopping and sit in the kitchen and watch Jen whip up things like homemade donuts, brownies, onion rings, and even flour tortillas.

Cooking would be an all-day event. On Saturday mornings, we would get up, and with plastic shopping bags in hand, we would set off to see what we could find in the local stores and at the bazaar. Our staple meal was the makings for a really good grilled cheese sandwich. A fresh loaf of white bread, a smoked gouda type cheese, butter, maybe some sausage, and a tomato slice if we could find it. My contribution to the weekend menu was a special snack consisting of small oyster type crackers (when we could find them) for dipping into sour cream that I would mix with my secret ingredient - taco seasoning (that my mom had sent me). The absolute height of sophistication, I know. It tasted good, proving the cliche was indeed true- Wisconsin people love their dairy products.

CHAPTER 10
YOU HAVE NEVER KNOWN TRUE BOREDOM

The true and utter boredom of my time in the Peace Corps is hard to describe. As far as I know, it is not something advertised in the Peace Corps brochures. No one talks about it. The hours and days and weeks of absolutely nothing to do but stare at the design on the wallpapered walls of my room. I can still vividly recall all four walls of my room covered in a dark beige wallpaper with a design printed on it that looked like those diagrams of the female reproductive system that you get in your junior high school health class. The boredom can be all-consuming. It can be so much that you become desperate for anything to happen, any kind of diversion. To pass the endless amount of free time, Jen and I played cards. Every night, and I mean every night without fail, we would gather in the evening to play card games, sometimes *Scrabble*.

Some activities bring some temporary relief from the boredom, like reading. Hours and hours of reading anything that you can get your hands on. I remember one special day as if it were a major holiday. The excitement. The anticipation. The pure joy of the big *TV Guide* Fall preview issue. I read it cover to cover. Everything from the descriptions of the made-for-tv movies coming up to what was happening on *Friends*. It was all there. The day my roommate received a stack of magazines in the mail is seared in my mind. It was a cold day, but the snow hadn't started yet. I oozed with jealousy. I cursed my family for not sending a similar package to me. "Why did my roommate get such a wonderful gift and not me?" I would moan. I just had to wait; my time would come. It wasn't a big package, but oh what joy it brought. The colors were almost blinding, so vivid. I never knew something so small could bring such joy. *People, Soap Opera Digest*, this would keep me busy until my turn came.

In silent agreement, Jen and I each took a few magazines and headed to our separate rooms. Snug under my five wool blankets, I read slowly and savored every word of those magazines. When the time was right, somehow, we knew or almost sensed that we were ready for an exchange. My excitement grew. Finally, it was here. The prized part of the package. My hands trembled as I touched the glossy cover, and my fingers traced the words, "*TV Guide* Fall Preview Issue." This was the mother lode. It wasn't just the *TV Guide*; this was the Fall Preview issue. The one source that would answer all my questions. Not only did this have a description of all the "made for tv" movies that were going to be shown for the whole season, but it also included hints at what was going to happen on my favorite shows. I was so desperate for entertainment that I bemoaned the fact that I was going to miss the *Sonny and Cher Story*, made for tv movie. I even spent a few minutes calculating if I left Ukraine/Peace Corps now, could I make it home for the *Sonny and Cher Story*. In the end, I stayed with only a small twinge of regret.

That was also the time Fred came into our lives. Fred was the dead fly hanging from a web on the ceiling light in the kitchen. Neither one of us bothered to clean the light of the cobweb, so instead, we named the poor guy Fred and would occasionally direct our frustration, boredom, and general malaise towards the dangling shell of an insect. He was a good listener. It occurred to me that some of the behaviors of myself, my roommate, and other volunteers could be warning signs that we were starting to lose it mentally. You get so used to how your everyday life is that you don't even realize how absurd it has gotten. I developed a few warning signs to look for:

1. You've given a name to the dead fly hanging from the ceiling light and have regular conversations with it.
2. You have started to wash out *Zip-loc* bags and hang them around the apartment to dry because you only have a limited supply of bags.
3. You have reread the *TV Guide* Fall Preview issue of the tv guide and consider it a prized addition to your literature collection.
4. You go shopping and find all the ingredients to make a really good sausage and cheese sandwich, and you talk about how good the sandwich was all week.
5. You decide that finding hair in your food and lipstick on your glass at a restaurant is all part of the ambiance.
6. You rush home every day to watch *Dynasty* (in Russian) on tv.
7. You no longer think it is odd for a kiosk to have vodka, black thong underwear, sausage, and laundry soap all in the same window. In fact, you are on a first-name basis with the women behind the counter because you have bought a Snickers candy bar there every day.
8. It's normal to do shots of vodka on a train trip using a camera film canister passed around among friends.
9. You impress your friends with your selection of *KoolAid* packets and discover that *Kool-Aid* and vodka make for a festive cocktail hour, or hours as the case may be.
10. When you see an old lady with a sack of potatoes getting on a bus, you wait for the next bus because nothing is worth the trouble of an old lady swinging a potato bag on public transportation.

The seemingly endless amount of free time gave plenty of time to contemplate...well, everything. From why that one boy was so mean to me in junior high school to what to do when I was done with Peace Corps. I couldn't go back in time and punch that boy from junior high in the face, but the possibilities were endless as far as when I finished my two years in Ukraine. Graduate school? Another stint in the Peace Corps? Open a bookstore in Key West? Wait. What? I had never been to Key West and knew nothing about owning a bookstore.

Nonetheless, nothing was off the table. The problem was I didn't know what I wanted to do. In Wisconsin, there was a fairly clear path to follow towards jobs and family, maybe buying a boat for fun-filled weekends on the lakes. Try as I might, it just wasn't a good fit for me. Now that I had decided not to go down that Wisconsin life path, I had to figure out what my path was. That unknown path with twists, turns and bumps that I was on was scary and exciting all at the same time, but I had plenty of time to sleep on it.

Boredom grew worse as winter set in. Below freezing temperature and a sunset that starts at about 4 p.m. is not conducive to going out and exploring the community. The only thing you want to do in those types of conditions is stay home and burrow down under the five wool blankets on your bed. Yes, you read that correctly. I had five wool blankets on my bed. Not only that, I usually slept in two layers of pajamas. That is not an exaggeration. It was that cold INSIDE our dorm rooms. Ukrainians would visit and ask why it was so cold in our rooms and put their hands on the radiators, feeling nothing with a very confused look on their faces. Students living in the same building often commented that it was so warm in their rooms that they would open their windows in below-freezing temperatures just to cool the room down. That most definitely was not our experience. We did what we could to combat the issue. The dorm ladies came in and sealed the windows up with strips of newspaper and some kind of paper mâché product. A couple of guys came to bang on the radiators, but it didn't change anything. Most winter nights, Jen and I would meet in our kitchen to play cards with wool blankets wrapped around ourselves to keep warm.

As you already know, I grew up in Wisconsin. A place not normally known for its balmy winter weather. The difference was that in Wisconsin, you lived in a heated house, got in a heated car, shopped at heated stores, and went to a heated work environment (for the most part). There are those crazy people that go fishing on a frozen lake in the middle of winter, but I never did understand the appeal of that. Having heat inside a building was a given in Wisconsin that I took for granted. This wasn't the situation in Ukraine. Going outside in the middle of winter involved trading multiple layers of sleeping attire for a different set of layers to go outside, usually three layers of clothes plus the required thick coat and boots. No turning on a heated car, no going into a heated grocery store, it was just cold everywhere, including our own home. Why would anyone want to go outside until the spring thaw?

Added to the extreme cold was the threat of the water being turned off that constantly hung over us and the Institute like a stubborn, ominous cloud. We had been told that the Institute had not paid their water bill in a long time, and there was no money to pay it. We would go long stretches with no hot water, but worse was when there was no water at all. At one point, all the students were sent home because the water had been cut off, and no one knew when it was coming back on. There was nothing for us to do, but stay home, buy bottled water, and constantly check the faucet for signs of life. The water situation didn't help combat the constant feeling of wanting to give up and go back to the States. It was indeed a battle of conflicting feelings. The cold and water issues were the norm for Ukrainians. For us Americans, it was almost a deal-breaker. One of my students said, "Americans know how to live, but not survive. Ukrainians know how to survive, but do not know how to live." It wasn't just one of my students that knew this saying; they all knew it. I am not sure if it was a widely publicized proverb, but it did put things into perspective. Giving up and going home was a constant battle for me.

CHAPTER 11
PUBLICITY TOUR

In the depth of winter snow covered the ground, which with all the people walking, it became packed-down ice on the roads and sidewalks, and then became one very long ice rink. No one shoveled sidewalks or roads, so getting anywhere was a hazard requiring sliding your feet and hoping not to fall. Oleksander, our coordinator, asked us to say a few words to some teachers that had gathered from the surrounding areas for a conference. This was a pretty common occurrence. When school had started, we had to meet with large groups of students from the English Department. Jen and I would sit in the front of the room, give a short speech then open it up for questions from the students. We were treated like honored guests, celebrities even. I had even put together a standard speech, opening with a joke, that could be used in almost any group meeting situation.

Ok, since you asked, my opening joke was: What do you call a person that speaks three languages? - trilingual. What do you call a person that speaks two languages? -bilingual. What do you call a person that speaks just one language? - (pause for contemplation) answer: American. I can't take credit for coming up with that, and I also have no idea who to give credit to. I did use it often, though, and it always got a chuckle. Proving the old adage, it's funny because it's true.

On this particular day, I was tired of being put on display in the name of Peace Corps and America, so I opted out when Oleksandr asked us to talk to this particular group of teachers. Jen, being the good volunteer, went to the meeting. She came back saying that we had been invited to a village to visit a school there and talk to the teachers. Repeating my motto, "I didn't have anything else to do," I agreed to go.

Jen and I didn't leave our dorm rooms very often. Trips out of our city were cumbersome. Similar to grocery shopping, traveling was a hassle. Buying train tickets (the main means of transportation between cities) was a complicated, almost impossible task. Tickets could only be bought at train stations in bigger cities. Buying tickets there involved standing for hours in line only to have the ticket booth close for "break time" as you waited. This forced everyone in line to frantically run towards the next open ticket window. After jostling for a place in line with other frustrated travelers, making it to the ticket window often resulted in rejection by the employee behind the glass. No tickets available. The Peace Corps office in Kiev even hired a person solely to solve logistical and transportation issues. This guy had connections to get any tickets or make arrangements for anything. It was the only way to do anything in Ukraine. You had to know someone.

We didn't even bother going into the city where we lived in the evening. Whether it was because we were content to stay inside in the evening or the warnings from various people telling us not to go into the city at night, I couldn't tell you what made us stay in so much. We were told Cafes in the city were hangouts for local mafia types and were to be avoided. The odd time when I did go out after dark, which happened because, in the middle of winter it started to get dark at 4 p.m., it was a rushed trip. Quickly walking the two blocks to the main square to buy bread. Keeping my head down and the collar of my coat pulled up, looking out for dangerous marauders when in reality, people were just trying to get home from work. The real issue with being out at night was drunk men harassing young women or an even bigger target- American women. So, we stayed home and made our own fun in the evening, mostly playing endless games of cards and *Scrabble*.

The visit to the village school was a few days after the conference. A car picked us up early in the morning, and we drove for what seemed like hours but was probably around two hours. We arrived in the smallest village I had ever seen in Ukraine. Granted, I hadn't traveled very much in Ukraine, but this place was a blink-and-you-miss-it town. Main Street consisted of two small square box-like buildings next to each other; the local grocery stores. I didn't ask at the time, but I wondered why two grocery stores, with basically the same items inside, were both open and working side by side. Did people have a preference for one store over the other? Did some families say, "I will only go to the store on the right," or did everyone go to both stores every time in case one store had something different? Hmmm. The never-ending questions, that is life in Ukraine.

As Jen and I were always on the lookout for hard-to-find items in the local stores, we went into both. The salespeople laughed as we said hello. I am not sure if it was because we greeted them in Ukrainian or because I had pulled a reusable shopping bag out of my coat pocket. In this village, as in a lot of cities and villages in Ukraine, they had never seen a foreigner, let alone one that said something in Ukrainian. The shelves in both stores were as empty as in our town, so we left with nothing in our ever-present plastic shopping bag. Next, we walked down to the house of a young couple, who were also teachers at the school, we would be visiting. They had been given a small house in exchange for teaching at the school. The husband had invited us to the school. We were offered a "tour" of the village and agreed, of course, although we were surprised because we thought we had already seen all the village had to offer. The next stop on the tour was the oldest house in the village. An authentic Ukrainian house with clay-like walls and a straw-thatched roof, like something out of a fairy tale. The owner of the house was an old lady, dressed in oversized, knee-high, black rubber boots, an oversized dark-colored coat, and a scarf wrapped over her head and tied at her chin. The haute couture fashion trend for babushkas in Ukraine. She invited us to take a look inside her tiny house. It was like stepping back in time. All the furniture and decorations were old Ukrainian. From the embroidered towels to the big wood-burning oven and the icons on the walls. The old lady told us that her father had died trying to save their land from being turned over to the Communists and run as part of a collective farm. I don't think this house had changed since before Communist times.

Moving on to the school, we were ushered into the school auditorium for the usual student performances that seemed to happen in every place we visited. It was a school talent show, of sorts, organized with students singing and dancing. The old English song *My Bonny Lies Over the Ocean* was a standard at these school shows. I wonder if during Communist times it was the only English song allowed in schools, because we heard it so often. Jen and I counted ourselves lucky that we didn't have to sit through another rendition of the Whitney Houston hit, *I Will Always Love You*. Another standard, for some unknown reason, in the school show repertoire. That particular song was usually an ear-splitting mess by a young girl that didn't know English and is singing phonetically with a heavy accent.

After the performances, the students were excused, and the teachers stayed for a Q&A session. Questions ranged from "Why we came to Ukraine?" to "Do we believe in Free Love?" That last question was a new one for us. The 1970s had just come to this tiny hamlet, I guess. Questions exhausted, it was time to eat and drink. We were led to the cafeteria with a big, long table filled with food and bottles of vodka. Toasts were made, food was eaten, vodka was consumed.

Giving a toast is extremely important at any gathering, large or small, in Ukraine. During training, it was suggested that we be prepared with a short speech or toast on these inevitable occasions. One of the Peace Corps admin coordinators would usually tell weird travel stories for his toast. The writer in our volunteer group would give poignant, literary toasts, sometimes with a poem that he had written, spoken entirely in Ukrainian. Ukrainian attendees at the gathering loved it and would fawn all over him. Really, who could make a toast after something like that? I had a standard toast: "I wish you peace, love, and happiness," a homage to my 1970's hippiness or "Here's to good friends, tonight is kind of special." (thank you, *Lowenbrau* commercial circa 1977). This was followed closely by an eye roll from any Americans that happen to be in the vicinity. Cliche, I know. I have no idea what made me think of that particular phrase, but it did fit most toasting occasions, and Ukrainians had never heard it.

The food was all homemade and delicious at the little village school reception. We ate well that night but did say a firm no to the jellied meat dish and the uncooked pig fat slices offered. After all the toasts were made and most of the food eaten, it was time to head home. Our hosts were happy and drunk. Just as I was looking at my watch, wondering when we were heading back, an overly intoxicated, middle-aged, overweight guy busted through the doors of the school cafeteria. The whole mood of the evening changed. Everyone was on edge. There was a lot of tension in the room. In the commotion of this drunk guy staggering around the cafeteria with a group of people surrounding him, trying to pacify and distract him, we were ushered outside to a waiting car. The drunk guy staggered outside too. He pushed people away, fixated on us and the car. We weren't sure what was going on until the teacher that was showing us around told us that the drunk guy was the head of the collective farm. He had given permission to use the car and provided gas for us to visit the school, and he was determined to give each of us a kiss. Jen and I quickly got in the backseat of the car and locked the door. Undaunted, the drunk guy pushed his way through people trying to block his way, unlocked the doors from the front, and lunged towards us. Despite our efforts to keep the door locked and scrambling towards the opposite side of the car, the guy was able to give each of us a kiss on the cheek. I felt we got off lucky. If this blowhard was this aggressive towards us, with a lot of people around, I can only imagine what this guy did to local women as he exerted his power over them. Our host tried to apologize for the guy and, in a polite way, said the guy was an asshole. A big understatement.

CHAPTER 12
I NEED A BREAK

When taking the train, there are two major worries before you even show your ticket to the conductor. The first is if your compartment is close to the bathroom and if the bathroom is going to be a toxic dumping site of epic proportion. If the compartment is close to the bathroom, you will have constant noise throughout the night as people move around and use the bathroom. Then there is the possibility that the smell from the bathroom will permeate the hall and into your compartment. These issues are of concern but don't normally stop a traveler from taking the train, which is the main transportation between major cities. Most people, including myself, enjoyed taking the train. The gently rocking motion as the train races down the track lulls you to sleep, and even the clanks and jolts of train car changes in the middle of the night didn't change my mind about this mode of transportation. I've had good and bad train experiences.

As part of pre-departure preparations, it is essential to gather the necessary food items that will sustain you for the overnight trip. A sampling of each of the four food groups is required. Those four food groups are the cheese and bread group, which is best when supplemented with sausage, the soda group- self-explanatory, the salty group; this includes chips, pretzels or crackers, and finally, the sweet or chocolate group. This final group includes my favorite - milk chocolate with hazelnuts - a must-have for any train trip, in my humble opinion. Now, for those purist that have the unnatural need for having fruit, go ahead, or go all out and add a few cucumbers and tomatoes for your sandwich too. To those health-conscious neophytes, I quote my father, who always says, "Do what you want, you are on vacation!"

Why interrupt the true hedonistic quality of a trip by having something that your mother would say is "good for you." Not having a representative of each of the four train food groups can be devastating to the whole train experience. Having too much can be a burden also. It can upset the delicate balance required for a successful trip. If you buy too much food, it means that you will have to carry that food around with you when you reach your destination or throw it away. I suggest allowing enough time before a trip to carefully pick out your train food. Some people will say they love to visit museums, and some say they want to see historical landmarks. As for me, I love to peruse local grocery stores. What better way to learn and explore the local culture than by seeing what the locals eat and buy? Trying to figure out what is inside the package is half the fun.

Finding all or even one of the items in these food groups was always a crapshoot in Ukraine. I don't need to mention the need for alcoholic beverages for the train ride. This mainly depends on who you are riding with. Traveling alone? You may want to be careful, depending on who your train compartment companions are. Two lovely Ukrainian women sharing my train compartment as we headed to Poland - me to meet my mother and them to buy things that they would bring back across the border for resale - offered me a libation during the ride. I declined but regretted that decision since it would have made the ride that much better.

This brings us to the most memorable trip to visit fellow volunteers, a few months after going to our individual sites. Jen, my roommate, wasn't going, I can't remember why. It was a holiday in Ukraine, which included students going home to celebrate and, more importantly, no classes. A bunch of volunteers took advantage of the holiday by having a gathering in one of the bigger cities in eastern Ukraine.

I started the journey solo. Ukrainian rucksack, bought at the local department store, on my back and heading to the town square to get a bus or taxi to the train station. It was morning, and my courage was at its peak for the day as I headed to the main square, which was a few blocks from my dorm. I was excited to meet up with friends and decompress from the daily frustrations of living in Ukraine. Everything dropped to an abysmal low a few minutes into the start of the trip as I reached the main square in town and saw an overstuffed bus pull away. There was absolutely no way for me to get on the bus; people were smashed up against the exit doors. Bus schedules didn't exist. When the next bus was coming was a question with no answer.

"No problem," I said to myself. "Taxi, it is," but all the taxies were gone, too. Frantically, I stuck my hand out, waving at oncoming traffic in a universal sign that I needed a ride. Nothing. On a side note, Ukraine had an unofficial and primitive *Uber* system. Flagging down a driver that happens to be going the same way was a great way for the driver to earn a few dollars and for the customer to avoid the woefully overcrowded transportation options. Alas, no cars pulled over. I didn't know how I was going to get to the train station. I started to panic. My weekend of fun, friends, and alcohol was in jeopardy. Out of nowhere, one of my students, Yuri, appeared at my side. For a moment, I thought this couldn't be a coincidence that he showed up that exact moment when I needed help. It seemed like everyone in town, and especially the Institute, was watching what the Americans were doing. Was it out of the realm of possibilities that today was Yuri's turn to rescue the distraught American as she tried to escape town? OK, maybe that is a little far-fetched, but how did one of my students know the exact moment to pop up at my side if no one was watching my movements? Or maybe I was starting to buy into the Communist propaganda of Big Brother watching you. After all, my roommate, Jen, was called a spy by a stranger on the electric train she was riding on when she told the guy she was a Peace Corps volunteer.

Conspiracy theories aside, I explained my situation to my student, Yuri, and seeing the panic on my face, he said, "I think I can help." I thought, "Great." What better person to hail a taxi or car than a local? I was wrong in a big way. Yuri threw my backpack over his shoulder and started walking. It took me a while to believe that Yuri's solution to my problem was to walk the five miles to the train station. I couldn't believe I was walking to the train station. The thought had never entered my mind that this was even a possibility. But walk we did, and at a pretty fast pace. I struggled to keep up with the pace of my student. Even without my backpack, I mainly walked behind him, trying to keep up. I kept thinking he would stop at one point and say, "Just kidding, let me flag down a car," but that never happened.

Yuri didn't even break a sweat the entire walk to the train station. I, on the other hand, was exhausted and ready to call it a day. Hey, I gave it a try, now time to go back and get back in bed. Bolstered by the excitement of a trip, I soldiered on and purchased the little scrap of paper they called a ticket for the electric train. The ticket was the size of a postage stamp but printed on thinner paper. Yuri had a look of confusion on his face as I stood in front of the ticket booth. No one bought tickets for the electric train. I am sure he thought it was some weird thing Americans do. I didn't want to tempt fate by not buying a ticket. It would be just my luck that if I didn't buy a ticket, the conductors would come through the train, and I would quickly get kicked off at the next stop, in the middle of nowhere, without a building in sight for miles. Amazingly, the train was waiting at the station when we walked to the platform. I felt I had walked into some alternate universe. This had never happened. No mad rush of pushing and shoving to get on the train. Yuri walked me to the train and handed over my backpack, so I must be getting on the correct train. I chose a window seat so could eat my Snickers candy bar and snooze leaning against the window, just how the electric train ride should be.

Three hours later, I arrived in Kiev. This was abnormal for an electric train ride. I had lost count of how many times the train was so crowded that I could barely get in the train door. Even if I made it in the doors, getting a seat on the electric train was like winning the lottery. Often, I had to stand in the train car breezeway between train cars. At each stop, as people got off and on, I would be slowly pushed towards the main seating area of the train car. One unfortunate time, I was stuck literally in the doorway of the train car. Not enough room for me to get into the main part of the car, and people behind me crowding me forward. Old ladies yelling at me when I got stuck exactly in the doorway. Yelling at me because the door was open, letting in a breeze, which is a gigantic no-no in Ukraine. A breeze or draft of any kind is strictly forbidden, as we all know a draft blowing will kill you.

After some pushing and shoving on the subway and walking a couple of blocks, I arrived at the Peace Corps admin office to meet up with two guys from my training group. My travel companions Peevo Bob and Bill #1., were already there, and I fell into a big group hug with them, so happy to see my fellow comrades. A wave of relief swept over me. Our merry trio wandered around Independence Square all day. Nothing to do until our train departed later that night. More walking, ugh. We browsed the tables of vendors selling souvenirs, and the guys drank beer. At about 10 p.m., we climbed on the train headed to Dnipropetrovsk. Peevo Bob, Bill #1 and I had the train cabin to ourselves. As soon as we were settled and on our way, Peevo Bob brought out the bottle of vodka. No cups, shot glasses, or containers that would hold liquid of any kind. What are a couple of Peace Corps Volunteers supposed to do? Not drink, go to sleep early, give up, and go home? No way, we were Peace Corps Volunteers!

After a quick search, Peevo Bob found a small, black plastic film canister, the approximate size of a shot glass. Perfect. The rest of the night was a blur of passing a film canister of vodka around our circle of trust and talking about our trials and tribulations. Long into the night, I almost kept up with my travel buddies. Almost being the keyword. My alcohol tolerance had grown exponentially in the few months I had been in Ukraine, but I was out of my league. Ok, I did skip a few rounds. These guys were on a whole different drinking level than me. They had been drinking beer while we were wandering around Kiev that day. Peevo Bob was the first to fall when he, without warning, stands up, stripped down to his tighty whities and white undershirt, and falls into the lower bunk. That left me and Bill #1 playing cards on the other bunk. For some reason, we decided to play gin rummy. I am sure it was my brilliant idea.

In my altered state, I was a math genius, keeping track of points, adding up cards, and generally being a card-playing savant, if only in my own mind. Bill #1 nodded along, agreeing with my every word, while also trying to sit upright. I tried to take advantage of Bill #1's intoxicated state to try to get the male perspective on my crushes and maybe get some insight into the male psyche. Bill #1 was too drunk to give any kind of coherent answer and even tried to say that I made out with a volunteer from the previous group at our end-of-training party. I think he was hoping I would make out with him right there in the train car with Peevo Bob passed out on the bench two feet away. I am only speculating but, come on, that is pathetic and a good reason to know when to call it a night. I soon succumbed to the alcohol and climbed into my top bunk for the night.

Morning arrived way too soon. A 6:00 a.m. train arrival time is a rude awakening, especially when the conductors start to wake people up at 5 a.m. Surprisingly or maybe not so surprisingly, Peevo Bob and Bill #1. were none the worse for wear. They were moving about our train compartment while I was still trying to figure out how to open my eyes... quietly. My head was splitting, and every move brought on a new wave of pain and spinning nausea as I struggled to pull my pants on over the long underwear I had slept in. There was a long line of people down the train car corridor, waiting for the bathroom. I took my place in line, bent over and clung to the handrail in the corridor, while also trying to maintain my balance as the train swayed back and forth. Yeah, that's me, just another foreigner riding the rails, nothing to concern yourselves with. Keep moving, people.

The stench of the bathroom hit me well before I got to the door. Closing the door behind me, I tried to figure out where to put my toothbrush, bottled water, and toilet paper in what was the size of a small closet—not wanting to touch anything in that tiny space. Although there was a tiny sink in the bathroom with running water, I wasn't willing to risk using the train water to brush my teeth. In fact, as a general rule, I would never use or drink the water coming out of the train bathroom faucet. The real challenge, drunk, hungover, or sober, is using the toilet. It takes talent and an incredible sense of balance. The toilet is about knee height, requiring a big step up to the top of the toilet. Despite being a squat toilet, it was not on the floor. I stepped up, putting my boots on the foothold and steadying myself by putting my hands on opposite walls of the bathroom and desperately trying to hold back the hangover nausea that was brewing inside me. Despite my multiple layers of clothes and the train rocking back and forth, I managed not to pee on myself or throw up. It's amazing what talents you develop while traveling.

The cold winter weather had settled in, but that morning, it was sunny and bright. The light hurt my red eyes, and the dark circles under my eyes looked like I had been in a fight and lost miserably. I was staying with my friend, Sherri, from training. She lived in a dormitory with a volunteer from another group. They lived in one big common room with two bedrooms and a kitchen attached to the main room. The smells of dogs (they both owned one) that weren't taken out as often as they should have added a layer of dreariness that was not only in their dorm rooms but the entire city. Those of us staying with Sherri and her roommate spent the daytime walking around the city. A big industrial, nondescript city.

Dnipropetrovsk is one of the biggest cities in Ukraine, and I was glad I didn't live there. Concrete, non-descript buildings everywhere, typical of the Soviet Era. Several volunteers were living in the city. Some were part of the small business development volunteers; others were English teacher volunteers in the local schools or at the University. Although there are benefits to having other volunteers living within fairly easy access, it was such a gray, depressing city that I was glad I didn't live there. It was also a very Russian city being in the eastern part of Ukraine. Ukraine is basically divided in half by the Dnipro River, running North to South down the middle of the country. Eastern Ukraine is heavily influenced by its border with Russia. Western Ukraine, despite its long history of moving border lines, has held onto its Ukrainian heritage and language. My very basic Ukrainian language knowledge was useless in eastern Ukraine. The response to my few words of Ukrainian was blank stares as Ukrainian and Russian are two completely different languages.

Later that night, the volunteers in the city gathered in one volunteer's apartment for our much anticipated and needed festivities. Only a couple of months had passed since training had ended. It was a long Ukrainian holiday weekend, and we were all super happy to get together to reconnect, talk, and mostly complain about what we had gone through since training had ended. Laughing, drinking, and general merriment was had by all. I met several other volunteers from other groups, along with a few Ukrainians brought by other volunteers and an American businessman or two. One middle-aged guy claimed to be the father of a semi-famous actor from a popular tv show. I had my doubts. Another volunteer spent the party ordering around his young Ukrainian fiancé. The poor girl was treated like a dog. Everyone noticed this asshole, and when they left, we gossiped about how this guy was treating some other poor girl the same way during training. I couldn't imagine marrying a Ukrainian guy, let alone putting up with what that girl did from an American asshole.

CHAPTER 13
SUDDENLY, THERE WERE COLORS

It didn't take long for Jen and I to start planning our first trip out of Ukraine. A month into living in Nizhyn and we were already studying our *Let's Go Europe* book like a Bible. Many nights were spent at the kitchen table, planning routes, places we would stay, and things we would do. We had heard some great things about Poland, specifically the city of Krakow, from other volunteers. This magical city was fairly easy to get to and had all the comforts we were looking for, American chain restaurants, movies in English, and inexpensive hotels.

The trip started with a late-night train from Kiev to Lviv. This was an overnight train, as most trains are in Ukraine. You get on in the evening and wake up in the morning at your destination. All train cars are sleeper cars; they have two or four beds, depending on which class you are in. They also have a third class that is an open train car but has beds for sleeping. With some help, we bought two seats in a second-class compartment.

It was close to midnight and two days before Christmas, and we were sitting in the overly crowded train station, waiting for our train to arrive. I was mesmerized by the crowds of people all carrying their giant bags. Worn out suit coats, older ladies in toe-pinching heals, each carrying a handle of an enormous plastic bag wrapped in rope to keep it closed. A layer of dirt and grim seemed to be everywhere, and the smell of body odor permeated the stagnant air. An occasional stray dog wandering around, hoping for a scrap of food. It was a surreal scene, considering Christmas last year was spent in the cozy embrace of my family and the chaos of laughter and everyone talking at once.

Finally, it was time to head to the train platform, and before we knew it, we were on our way with the conductor giving us our bedsheets and asking us if we wanted tea. Luckily, we had the compartment to ourselves. The major problem was the window was stuck open, with about a five-inch gap, bringing fresh air and also made the compartment freezing cold. It was December, and while this might be a welcome sight on a hot and humid summer night, it was disheartening for the beginning of a mid-winter excursion. We couldn't get the window closed. The conductor gave it a try but threw up her hands in the universal sign of tough luck.

It was a long night, trying to stay warm, sleeping fully clothed with coats, hats, and mittens, while also ignoring the sounds of the train car. Unfortunately, we were also close to the train car's bathroom. The constant opening and closing of doors and people moving around added to a lack of sleep because we had kept our compartment door open in a vain effort to let some of the warm train car air into our compartment. Arrival came early to the city of Lviv. Already, just being in this city, things seemed a little brighter. The cobblestone streets and old stone buildings with tall windows and balconies allowed the imagination to travel back in time. Thankfully, the big Soviet concrete apartment monstrosities were pushed to the outside of the city. We took a taxi to the Hotel George, in the center of the city, where we were supposed to meet Bill #2, a fellow volunteer from our group. We sat down in the lobby of the hotel, a throw-back to another era. Marble floors, floor-to-ceiling marble columns framed the massive, curved staircase with a red carpet. We sat ourselves and our bags on two chairs in the ornate lobby, knowing it would probably be a long haul. We had no way of communicating with Bill #2, so we could do nothing but wait. We waited and waited and waited. We weren't sure what to do, not sure what had happened to Bill #2. After several hours, we decided to get a room for the night because we had no way of contacting the other volunteers that were living in Lviv.

As soon as we got into the room and freshened up, there was a call at the front desk for us. Another volunteer from our group called the hotel to tell us that Bill #2 wasn't coming and that we should come to their apartment. The volunteer was a sweet lady named Halia that spoke fluent Ukrainian and had relatives that lived in Ukraine. Her husband, Ted, was an equally nice business volunteer. Halia explained to the hotel people that we wouldn't be needing the room after all, and Ted, her husband, came to meet us.

After a brief rest at Ted and Halia's apartment, we headed to a Chinese restaurant for Christmas Eve dinner. About ten of us sat at the restaurant, ready for a feast. I was excited not to have Ukrainian food. A Chinese restaurant was definitely out of the ordinary, especially where we were living. We ordered and chatted, happy to be together. Just before the food was served, the electricity suddenly went out. We sat in total darkness, unfazed; this was Ukraine, after all. We made the best of it, laughed, and sang Christmas carols until the lights came on again.

Halia and Ted had the keys to another volunteer's apartment while he was away, so they offered to let Jen and I stay there. It was the apartment of the young woman chaser from our training group. Jen and I were a little apprehensive about what we would find at his apartment, but hey, it was a free place to stay, and we didn't plan on looking too closely at our surroundings, afraid of what we might find. It was a spacious one-room apartment with two fold-out sofas/beds and a grand piano, of all things, right in the middle of the main room. Next to the beds was a large gas heater. It was a large cement floor-to-ceiling tower with ceramic tile, and little doors to light the gas nozzle. Neither one of us had any idea how to light the gas heater, so Ted started it before he left and told us the apartment should warm up soon. The place was unbelievably cold. I was excited for the room to heat up to a nice cozy level. I had grown very tired of living in the icebox, otherwise known as our dorm rooms. I was on vacation, and all I wanted was a nice warm place to relax. While waiting for the room to warm up, I checked out the water situation. A warm shower would have washed the dirt of the day off. I made a beeline for the bathroom and turned on the faucet in the tub. I almost cried as I frantically turned both faucets to full blast, but all that came out was a small trickle.

As in most cities in Ukraine, the water was turned off at night to save money. I didn't spend any time mourning the loss because I was anticipating sleeping in the cozy bliss of warmth. I was exhausted, and we had to get up fairly early for the next leg of our journey toward Poland. The room still wasn't heating up, and the cold was unbelievable. We had no clue how the heater worked, so we ended up sleeping not only fully clothed but also wearing winter coats, mittens, and hats. I even kept my boots on. Freezing all night and not sleeping much.

After gathering all the inside information on traveling to Poland, we were headed out with a slight change in our passenger list. Bill #2 was sick and wasn't meeting us, but Frank joined our travel group instead. Frank was a volunteer from the business group. Slightly aloof and prone to wandering off to explore. The first leg of our journey was a train to the Polish border. We ended up in a third-class car, a train car that was dirty with broken windows and graffiti. Yet again, we were freezing. Or should I say a thawing out had never occurred? Except for a young Ukrainian guy with a big bag in the seating area next to us, the train car was empty. I can't say for sure, but I think there were only a few cars on our train. We didn't explore, hoping the ride would be a short one. Besides, the chances of an Orient Express type dining car were slim.

A couple of hours later, we were at the border. Polish guards came onto the train to check passports. The guards were probably wondering why the Americans were traveling on a train that was practically just a shell of a train car but didn't ask anything, just checked our passports. The young guy next to us, however, was having a rough day. Not only did the guards give him a hard time, but they went through his bag and made him pull down his pants, revealing his stash of illegal vodka bottles and cigarettes he was trying to get across the border. After surrounding the poor guy and some subdued discussion between the guards, they took him off the train, and we continued toward the Polish border.

Passing the border into Poland was like Dorothy entering the Emerald City. It felt like we were seeing colors for the first time. Everything was brighter, softer, and just beautiful. We were a few miles into Poland, and happiness fell over our little band of travelers. At the border train station, we managed to buy train tickets to Krakow and waited until early evening when our train arrived in a nice, mostly clean train station. No old ladies with huge sacks of potatoes or drunk guys sitting around playing cards and yelling. Showing our tickets to the conductor, we stepped on the most beautiful train we had been on in a long time, if ever—airplane-type seats with headrests and plenty of legroom. We were so excited to just be a couple of hours away from Krakow. We sat back and relaxed, enjoying the luxury as the sun went down.

We knew it would take about 2-3 hours to get there but didn't know exactly when we would arrive or if that was the final destination of the train. An hour or so into the ride, we started to get anxious about getting off at the right place. At one point, the train made a long stop at a train station. We had no idea where we were. It was dark outside, and we couldn't see anything outside the train. After sitting at the station for about 15 minutes, it got ready to go again, but this time it went backward. Back in the direction we had just come from. Jen and I looked at each other in a panic. Frank sat unfazed. Jen pops up and runs through the train car, looking for a conductor. Somehow, she managed to explain to the conductor our predicament, and he checked the train schedules. Through a series of hand gestures and pointing, the conductor tells us to get off at an upcoming stop. At that stop, the next train that stopped at the station was going to Krakow.

The conductor gave us a nod, and we reluctantly stepped off the train and onto a platform in the middle of nowhere. Let me repeat, we were literally in the middle of nowhere, somewhere in Poland. At least, we knew we were in Poland, but that was about it. The train continued on its route as we stood on a huge concrete platform, watching it disappear into the darkness. We put all our faith in the conductor and the information that he had communicated to us. A few streetlights lit the platform, but otherwise, it is dark and quiet. Several hundred feet away were a few kiosks and a cafe with lights and loud techno music. Nothing else around for miles and miles. Frank being Frank wanders off toward the lights and is soon out of sight. We joke about his wandering off and even call his name, but it's clear he is out of shouting distance. Frank does eventually wander back, and we ask where he was, and typically, he answers, "Just wanted to see what was over there."

We waited on that platform just long enough to question our initial decision to get off the train. Did the conductor really say another train would be coming, or did he say it wouldn't be coming and we needed to get off the train anyway? Before long, we see the big, round light of a train headlight coming down the track. We are nervous because the conductor told us that the train only stops for a minute. We have to hop on with all our luggage (still haven't learned the whole packing light thing). It was going to be a challenge. Jen and I grab a piece of luggage in each hand and step closer to the edge of the platform. The train chugs closer and closer as we adjust the grip on our bags. We remind ourselves of the short timeframe to get on the train. Frank, of course, is oblivious to our anxiety. Closer, closer, the horn blares get louder, and my heart races. Then, WHOOSH! A single train engine races past us at a speed so fast that it sends a gust of wind over us, blowing our bags and slapping us in the face. We stand in shock and horror as it zooms past us. It takes a full minute to register what has happened before Jen and I lose it. Dropping out bags, we double over, laughing so hard I can't breathe. If I could have rolled on the ground, I would have. It was the laughter of people that have totally and completely lost it.

The uncontrollable laughter continues for a least five minutes until we remember how we must have looked and start laughing again. Except for Frank, who is looking at us, not quite understanding what we find so hilarious, who decides to wander off towards the cafe again. Recovery is slow from the absurd situation of getting ready to board a train that was never going to stop. It was like a scene from a 1980's John Cusack teen movie. You know the one where John Cusack is in pursuit of the girl of his dreams and gets in many comedic and outlandish situations.

Eventually, another train does come, and this one stops. We pull ourselves and our luggage up the train steps and walk down the car, looking for open seats. This train has compartments with four seats on both sides. It is a busy train, full of European teens and backpackers. We felt like we were heading in the right direction. We managed to find seats together in one compartment and lift our luggage, with some help, into the overhead racks, then wait. The conductor comes through to check tickets and is confused by our tickets from another train. He doesn't speak English but does manage to tell us we have to pay more to ride on the train. Not wanting to get off the train again, we pay.

CHAPTER 14

THOSE BEAUTIFUL GOLDEN ARCHES

Finally, the train enters a large city, and we know we are getting close. It's late evening. We are giddy with excitement, exhaustion, and possess a one-minded determination to reach our destination. Even Frank had an almost imperceptible change in his demeanor. No need to even talk; without words, we communicated what we wanted most. The train rolls into the station, and we were ready. Bags in our hands and heavy backpacks strapped to our backs, barreling down through the dark station, old women and small children be dammed, we were on a mission. Blocking out all sites, sounds, and smells, our minds became focused on just one thing. Never mind that Jen and I had been traveling for two days, and we were tired and hadn't taken a shower since we left home. Nothing mattered except reaching the goal. It had been seven long months since any of us had seen those beautiful golden arches. We blindly followed the glow of that beautiful yellow light on a spiritual journey towards warmth and enlightenment. I felt a part of me had been missing for so long, and now... now, I could be whole again.

We walked in the door, and a burst of warm air rushed towards us. I closed my eyes for a second and let the smells invade my senses. In a daze, we moved forward, drinking in the sights and sounds. Making our way to the counter, we heard those magical words we had longed to hear, "Welcome to *McDonald's*. Can I take your order, please?" Ok, she said them in Polish, but I felt the meaning behind those sweet words deep in my soul. My mouth went dry, and I grabbed the counter to steady myself. I now knew this wasn't a dream. Somehow my mouth formed the words I had been practicing for months, "I'll have a *Big Mac*, please!"

As if by magic, the food appeared in front of me. I looked up with breathless anticipation and said, "Thank you," for that was all I could think of to say. How could I ever show my appreciation for what they had given me? I quickly found a table and sat down. For a moment, I just stared at my tray. I tried to wait for Jen and Frank to join me at the table, but a sense of urgency came over me. I brushed back a tear and unwrapped my *Big Mac*. I couldn't take it anymore. I leaned back my head, closed my eyes, and silently screamed, "Yes, Yes, Yes!"

Like a silent prayer vigil, we all sat and concentrated on the feast set before us. Every morsel was cherished. The angels sang in the background, or was that the European techno music coming from the speakers? It didn't matter. I was in the place I had been dreaming about for months. Hallelujah and praise to the American fast-food gods. With the final licking of my finger, I stumbled outside in the brisk winter night, and in my post-fast-food stupor, noticed that the twinkly lights were brighter, the air was crisper, the stores more enticing, and all was well with my world.

What is it about McDonald's in a foreign country that just makes everything better? Not just the food; that is always the same as you would get at home. But also the friendly faces of the employees and the magnificently clean bathrooms fully stocked with toilet paper. Clean, shiny, and a little piece of home. For those of you that have traveled internationally, you know what I mean. As long as there is a McDonald's, you can be assured of some good food and immaculate bathrooms. It makes a difference when a clean bathroom is easy to find, and you often find yourself mapping out your route according to the location of McDonald's. For those of you that refuse to admit you go to McDonald's, we see you slinking in a side door to use the bathroom or maybe the free internet.

CHAPTER 15
BACK TO MY NEW REALITY

O ur time in Krakow was magical. Movies in English (with Polish subtitles), chain restaurants (*Pizza Hut*, *Wendy's*), even an Italian and Chinese restaurant, it doesn't get much better than that. Everything was at our fingertips, and we loved it. Jen and I had a couple of drinks in a local bar, and a French guy followed us back to the hotel. Jen took charge and told the guy to leave. Add French to the list of languages I do not know. It wasn't all frivolous abandon. We managed to take in some of the local sights and souvenir shopping. Also took a day for a tour of Auschwitz-Birkenau Concentration camps. A sobering experience, to say the least. The tourist bus to these locations was cordial with polite chitchat, compared to the sober, contemplative silence of the ride back to Krakow. An experience that changes everyone.

A couple of other volunteers met us in the same hotel we were staying in. Kathleen, Opal, Sherri, and Marie came for the New Year's celebrations and to indulge in all that Poland had to offer. The central square on New Year's Eve was a riot of drunk people walking around, setting off firecrackers, sometimes into the crowd. We all ended up in our hotel room drinking champagne and celebrating the New Year because the overly excited crowd was a little intimidating. Seeing our training group mates was almost a mini Peace Corps three group reunion.

Two days later, Jen and I tried to mail some things home from the local Polish Post Office since we had heard it was easier than trying to mail things from Ukraine. And for the most part, it was. Unfortunately, they wouldn't accept the beautiful painting I had bought in Kiev on Ukrainian Independence Day. I loved my oil painting that was impressionistic in dark romantic hues. I had bought it from this handsome man with shaggy blonde hair and stunningly green eyes. What is with my attraction to green-eyed artist types? Sigh. I digress. I haggled a little, and the painting was one of my prized possessions. However, I didn't have the right paperwork, so I had to bring it back with me to Ukraine. Amazingly, I didn't damage the framed painting with all the trains and hostels during that trip.

After New Year's, Jen and I bought tickets for a train heading to Prague in the Czech Republic. I didn't know much about our destination, but what I did hear sounded promising. History, culture, beauty, and food; doesn't take much to entice me. This time, we got on the right train and went to yet another Polish border. Due to train schedules, we had a several-hour wait at the border train station in the middle of the night. We waited in the dimly lit station alongside a large number of fellow travelers from all over the world, sprawled on the floor with their backpacks and sleeping bags. For reasons I couldn't fully understand, people were willingly traveling to Eastern European countries. I was just beginning to realize the whole travel urge/addiction thing. Why people would willingly leave the nice clean, civilized comforts of Western Europe or Australia was beyond my comprehension. To me, Western Europe was sleek and modern with cool people that lived in minimalistic apartments and spoke several languages. I wonder if I had thought to ask these fellow travelers why they were going to Eastern Europe if their answers would have been similar to the reasons I left Wisconsin.

Our second train to Prague started in the middle of the night, and we had chosen a non-sleeping class train car to save money. Luckily, the seats reclined a little, so we tried to get some sleep during the long ride to Prague.

The first order of business, upon arrival, was finding a place to stay. The always handy *Let's Go Europe* book said there was a hostel right in the train station. Well, not inside the train station, more like going outside and walking around the building to a separate entrance in the same building. So, off we went. Finding the place was fairly easy, but the real obstacle was mustering the energy to climb the eight flights of spiral stairs to get there—eight floors with four sets of stairs on every floor. At the bottom, we looked up the open stairway with the stairs winding around it and groaned in unison—an all-new form of torture was above us. We needed a place to stay, so our ascent began. Out of breath after the first set of stairs, I wondered if it would be ok if I just dumped my backpack of clothes off the third-floor landing, left for someone else to deal with. Not even half-way up, I was wheezing and panting and couldn't even muster the energy to joke about this absurd predicament. I wondered which floor they kept the bodies of the people that didn't make it to the top floor. Hearts pounding and unable to speak, we made it up to the top floor. As we reached the reception desk, we wondered how many people, if not all, arrived at the same desk so winded they couldn't speak. It took a full five minutes of heavy breathing until we could ask about a room. We opted for the women's only group room, which turned out to be clean and not too bad for sleeping purposes. A bunch of twin beds and bunk beds scattered around one large room. Dropping our bags off, we headed out to the city after double-checking we had what we needed for the day. There was no way in hell I was going up those stairs for anything forgotten.

We did the usual tourist things. Walking across the St. Charles Bridge, watching the clock chime on the hour in the main square, and wandering through souvenir shops. We had heard that pot was legal in Prague but didn't venture into the shops that sold it. As with the culture of most hostels, our fellow travelers were friendly, and one or two even went with us on sightseeing jaunts.

One morning as the girls in our room were waking up and starting their day, our eyes were drawn to a decidedly masculine-looking woman in one of the beds snoring loudly. All of us looking at each other, wondering what was going on, because he hadn't been there the night before. The person did eventually wake up looking around with all eyes on him as he sheepishly left the room as we giggled.

As all vacations must come to an end, so must ours, and we got on a train headed back to Kiev. This time, it was a direct train, no changing trains in the middle of nowhere. It was a long, long train ride, 24 hours. We passed the time alternating between sleeping and a lot of reading, and we had snacks, of course, because we not uncivilized.

Before I knew it, the second semester started, and sometime after that, our actual classes started. Everything was the same as the first semester. Long hours of nothing to do interrupted by teaching and letters from home and cooking on the weekends. Sergey, one of the fifth-year students (aka- movie boy or movie Sergey), resumed his weekly visits to our rooms, regaling us with descriptions of American movies that he had seen the previous weekend. We could always count on him for a laugh and animated conversations.

It was about this time that my host brother showed up at our door unexpectedly. I was dumbfounded. He said his mother wanted him to check up on me and had also brought some homemade food. I invited him in, and the extremely awkward visit began. What was I supposed to do with the guy? Jen and I were not tea or coffee drinkers, so I couldn't be the typical Ukrainian host. I had nothing to offer my guest besides water. I didn't think he would appreciate the day-old bread we had on the shelf, the only food we had available at the time. Adding to all that awkwardness was my Ukrainian was the same if not worse than during training, and his English was still limited. Jen, for some reason, stayed in her room during this whole ordeal, which only added to the uncomfortable situation. We stumbled through a basic conversation. When I asked about Andre (the friend that I had met), my host brother's face turned to stone with a thin straight line where his mouth used to be. My host brother slowly told me that Andre had been in a car accident and had died a few months ago. Well, there goes the beautiful children that Andre and myself were supposed to have. Pass the tissues, please. A reminder to grab hold of opportunities right away, before it's too late.

Dima, my host brother, did not get the hint that this was a weird encounter as he lingered around even after I said I had to teach my classes. I brought him to the Institute and pawned him off on Oleksander to get a tour of the Institute. After that, I sent him on his way back to Kiev. I felt a little bad about sending him away, but a forced friendship only created more uncomfortableness.

Writing letters home was always on the day's agenda. Before I left for Ukraine, I decided that I would write one letter to everyone that had come to my going away party and various friends and family. Then I would only respond to letters that people had written to me. Letters from home were always anxiously awaited. Usually, mail got to us through Oleksander, our coordinator. This meant that it was slow getting to us because we had to wait for him to check in with the ladies in the mail office in a separate building. A couple of months in, Jen found the mail office at the Institute. After I heard about this little bit of information, I would wait outside the office until it opened to check for letters. Almost every day, I was pacing outside the office, waiting for the mail lady to finish her break. Slowly, I wore a groove in the hardwood floor outside that little office. I was starved for letters from home. This was a time before I knew what email was. Handwritten letters could take two, three, or more weeks to arrive. It was torture to wait that long to get a little tidbit of what was happening at home. When my grandfather passed away, I didn't know it until three weeks later. Then I had to say goodbye and pass on my condolences via another three-week lag in communication. I get it, people were busy, and life had gone on at home without me there. I had taken off to explore the world, but that didn't mean I didn't get homesick. That I still didn't wonder what I was missing out on at home. I needed that connection to family and friends at home and going any length of time without letters from home was torture. The only thing I could do was make the letters I wrote home as interesting as possible to entice the recipient to respond. Given my life in Ukraine was so different, it didn't take any embellishment of true-life events. One friend even commented that my "letters were so funny." My unwritten response was, "But that is my real life."

I spent a lot of time responding to letters. Trying to add interesting stories or tidbits to letters so that the recipient would be compelled to respond. The letters I worked the hardest on were letters to Jake. Yes, you read that correctly. Jake, my crush, the man I had lusted after for ... a long time, and I had exchanged a few letters over the months. Not a lot, because the mail took forever, and I stuck to my rule of not writing unless I received a letter. Jake's parents gave the first clue of a coming letter from Jake when they sent a card that said: "Don't be surprised if Jake writes to you." A simple line that I quickly forgot because I didn't think it would happen. Jake didn't seem like the letter-writing sort. Although I had never said the words that I was interested in Jake to anyone, my inept attempts to get Jake's attention were obvious to anyone within a mile radius, even his parents—embarrassing on many levels. I had followed Jake around like a puppy hoping for attention. As for what Jake thought of me, I can only guess. I'm sure he liked having a girl thirteen years younger than him mooning over him, but he was never interested enough to ask me out or be anything more than a friend.

The arrival of the first letter from Jake was a shock. I eagerly read and re-read his letter. Two pages of hard-to-read chicken scratches with little real information. For the next couple of days, I would re-read and try to digest the letter. The typical girl reaction, I analyzed every word and dissected possible meanings. "You are missed" could be interpreted in so many ways. Does that mean he missed me or that the rest of the crew wondered where that dark-haired, quiet chick was? Errr, the angst of trying to navigate the world of men. What's a girl to do but soldier on and flirt via snail mail. Having mulled a response in my head for a few days, I was ready to put pen to paper. After careful consideration of his words, I would start to compose my response. First, I would set the mood. Going to my room and playing a cassette tape of my favorite Bonnie Raitt or Melissa Etheridge songs. Then carefully printing in precise handwriting, I would pour all my creative energy into a response that was both inquisitive (so that he had questions to respond to) and also filled with stories of my trials and tribulations. Sometimes, rewriting letters to get the exact tone I wanted. Somehow trying to convey my affection for him, but not being too over the top. Ahh, the delicate dance of a one-sided infatuation from half a world away.

CHAPTER 16
ARE YOU LEAVING TOO?

The day started like any other day. Sleeping in. Getting ready to teach my class. No rush. It was spring, and things outside were beginning to become brighter. Jen had started to say that she was ready to go home, but for some reason, I didn't believe her until that day. Probably because I didn't want her to leave. We had become close friends. So close that we would finish each other's sentences, and one word or look would send us into endless laughter. At a Peace Corps volunteer conference, the other volunteers looked at Jen and I like we had been in-country too long and may be in need of some physiological intervention. Staring at us while we laughed until tears rolled down at some inside joke. Like the time Jen and I wrote notes of religious proclamations on the shower room tile, *Post-it* notes attached to an icon picture hung in the bathroom someone had given us, and messages written in the container of butter. Telling people that my roommate wrote "Repent, you sinner" in a tub of margarine isn't as hilarious as experiencing it yourself. Trust me. Sizing us up for strait-jackets was a logical conclusion to seeing Jen and I laughing at our own jokes. I was hoping for a nice light pastel color in a size large rather than XL- the repetitious food availability was getting to me.

Anyway, as I was getting ready for my classes that particular day, I was in the hallway brushing my teeth when I noticed some drips on the floor. No clothes had been recently washed with the resulting steady stream of water down the hallway from poorly wrung out jeans, so I knew that wasn't the cause of the water on the floor. Curious, I looked up at the ceiling light and noticed some water dripping from it. Hmmm. Before I could get out the words, "Jen, look at this," water started streaming out of the light fixture. Looking around at a second room, water was freely flowing out of that ceiling light too. Even the light switches on the wall had water coming out.

I ran down the hallway, looking for the ladies that watched the front desk area of the building, using a variety of hand signals and rudimentary language skills to get the ladies to follow me back to our rooms. Jen started moving beds, carpets, and other things in the way of the free-flowing water, grabbing anything that could hold water and using it to contain the flood. Soon, we had several of the women from the front reception area in our rooms repeatedly saying, "Oh my God," before scrambling to find the source of the water leakage. It turned out to be the dorm rooms above us. The water had been turned off earlier that morning (this happened periodically, it was Ukraine after all), and the woman above us had turned on all the faucets, forgetting about it and left to teach her classes. All we could do was sit and wait while the water was turned off and the mess cleaned up. Because the water was coming through light fixtures and switches, it would need a few days to dry out before we could stay there again. Jen and I packed our bags and headed to Kiev. A little Peace Corps sponsored respite from our site. Since we had no place to live, we could stay in the Peace Corps apartment they had for volunteers in Kiev for business reasons.

The reality of Jen leaving hit hard during this trip. Jen took the opportunity of us being in Kiev to tell our Peace Corps coordinator that she wanted to leave. I didn't believe it was real until that day. I dreaded being alone and didn't want my friend to leave. The only other person at the Peace Corps apartment was Bill #2. A volunteer from our group that was heading home. Not sure the exact circumstances of his leaving, but there was a young woman in Kiev to see him off. What exactly that meant, I didn't ask. Bill #2, Jen, and I hung around eating at restaurants and hanging out at the apartment. There was a lot of waiting around for paperwork to process. On the evening before Bill #2 left and with surprisingly no alcohol involved, we came up with an extensive and not very politically correct list of alternative Peace Corps slogans. Among them - Peace Corps, the toughest job you won't really like- was one of the more tamer slogans. Our jaded attitude was really towards the difficult struggle of living in Ukraine. It was close to Easter, but as we sat at one restaurant, a Christmas song that I had never heard before, in English, came over the speaker system. Somehow, this seemed appropriate and summed up our time in Ukraine. Things were just backward in Ukraine, and not much made sense.

After a few days of relaxation, we went back to Nizhyn. Jen started her preparations for leaving in late spring. I didn't know what I was going to do. I wasn't ready to leave and didn't have anything to go home to. I already had plans to go home for a visit in the summer, so I would finish out the semester at the Institute. I wasn't going to quit now, although I thought long and hard about it.

This was also when the questions started. Students, fellow volunteers, even people I thought were friends asking, "Are you leaving too?" Or worse, "What are you going to do without Jen?" It became annoying. Is that what people thought about me, that I couldn't possibly survive without Jen? I thought I was a different person than I had been in Wisconsin. Maybe not drastically changed, being a quiet person is a lifelong affliction, but changed a little at least. Changed enough that I was my own person capable of following through with my decision to work for the Peace Corps. People naturally went towards Jen as the leader of our duo. It just wasn't part of who I was to take the lead. Sure, I had taken the giant leap to leave my life in my hometown and also put behind me the ingrained perception, by those around me at home, of who I was as a person. By taking this different path, I met people that didn't know who I was back in my hometown. I guess I was working under the delusion that I was becoming my real self, but the question was, what did other people see?

I often wondered what my experience would have been like if I had been sent to a site by myself. No roommate to share the hardship and endless laughter or, worse, assigned a roommate that I didn't get along with. That easily could have been the case. When the Peace Corps admin people were making their site placements, four of us were asked about rooming together. Jen and I both chose each other. Not that we didn't like or get along with the other two volunteers, it came down to personality, compatibility and smoking preferences. Now that Jen was leaving, I would be on my own, the only Peace Corps volunteer at my site, institute, and city. Oh wait, that wasn't the way things worked out.

A few days before Jen left, I got a call from the Peace Corps office. They wanted to put another volunteer from our group, Opal, into Jen's place in Nizhyn. I said, "Yes," of course. I wanted the company. I knew Opal from our training group. We had hung out in the same group of friends together during training, so I thought things would work out. Opal had to leave her site in eastern Ukraine for environmental concerns. She had been assigned a town whose name translates to "Yellow Water" and had an open Uranium mine - I'm surprised Opal wasn't pulled out earlier.

A tearful goodbye to Jen as she headed back to the States. A few days later, I went to Kiev to help Opal move her belongings to Nizhyn. The dynamics changed at the Institute with the arrival of Opal. I knew how things worked and was the person people were used to seeing. I became the main contact for Oleksandr, our coordinator, who had a preference for me to speak instead of Opal because I didn't have a thick southern accent. A preference solidified when Oleksander asked me to make a recording of myself reading a book he selected. He set up a recording session with ancient equipment that took up a whole wall in a room I had never seen before at the Institute. In the first and only session, I made it about halfway through the book. It's harder than you would think to read something through without stumbling over words and your voice getting tired. Guess I will never be a voice-over actress.

We coasted through the end of the semester. Opal was an ok roommate with only a few annoying habits, but we didn't have the closeness that Jen and I had. Going to prom with an older divorced guy and her parents getting married at age 13, Opal embodied a rural southern stereotype. Her thick southern accent and funny stories of her family and rural life back in Alabama were always good for a laugh. Later on, the roommate compatibility would turn into me trying to placate Opal because I felt guilty about moving in a different direction that didn't include her, but more on that later.

CHAPTER 17
WHERE AM I?

Before I flew home for a short respite of sorts, I made plans to meet my mother in Poland and travel around a bit. We were able to talk on the phone a few times, making plans to meet at a hotel in Warsaw. Not having the language ability or access to the complicated train ticket purchasing windows at the train station, I asked a trusted student to buy the ticket for me. He was able to get me a direct train, Kiev to Warsaw. Whew, one less travel hassle, or so I thought.

Heaving my overstuffed backpack on the train, I found my cabin and stowed my backpack under the seat. I had overpacked my bag, as usual, which is ironic since it was summer, and for whatever reason, I didn't have shorts to wear. I was used to wearing many, many layers to get through the cold winter months. Switching my limited clothing options to summer-related clothes was somehow more difficult. I packed too many warm clothes and not one pair of shorts. Later, I would end up cutting off the legs of a pair of sweatpants with hideous results. Good thing I didn't know anyone in Europe. There I go again, getting off-topic. Back to the train departure.

I took my book out and waited to see who my cabin mates would be. I was traveling alone for the first time. Nervous and trying to quiet the voices in my head, asking, "What the hell are you doing traveling alone?" and "You don't speak the language, and not only are you a woman traveling alone but an American woman traveling alone. Are you looking for trouble?" There were three open seats in my compartment. I crossed my fingers that I wouldn't find myself stuck with a group of men drinking bottles of vodka all night and generally harassing any woman that happens to cross their path. I had heard stories and was on guard, but not sure what I was going to do if faced with that kind of situation. It was a relief to see two 30ish-year-old women with hair dyed the same red color, the same red color as most women in the former Soviet Union had (Soviet Union red #1962), uncomfortable-looking strappy heels, and several bags busting at the seams with things to sell in Poland. They could tell I was a foreigner, and after my basic language skills were exhausted, they set up their food and drinks on the little table next to the window of our train cabin. They offered me shots of cognac, and I offered my can of Planters cheese curls. We amicably carried on our trip as the train bumped along into the night.

In the middle of the night (it's always the middle of the night in these types of situations), the train slowed and stopped. Listening to the commotion of heavy boots and men's voices outside and in the hallways of the train cars, it was obvious that we were at the border crossing. Sleepily, I sat up, got my passport out from my neck pouch, and waited for the guards to come to our compartment. Soon, the uniformed guards with their sidearms, utility belts, and rifles slung over their shoulders came to our door. The two women in my compartment gave their passports to the guard. He quickly swiped through the pages and gave the passports back. I gave my passport to a stocky guard with a blond crew cut, and he flipped through the pages with a dollar sign tattooed index finger. Then he slowly swiped through the pages a few more times as though he was looking for something specific.

The guard looks at me, and after realizing I didn't speak Russian, says to me in English, "You have no visa in your passport." Very confused, I stand up next to the guard asking why I need a visa. We go back and forth a few times with him saying, "You don't have a visa," and me saying, "Why do I need a visa?" Until in the middle of our debate, I glance at the top of the sleeve of his uniform. There, on the patch on his shoulder, I sounded out the word "B-e-l-a-r-u-s" written in Cyrillic. Until that precise moment, I thought I was in Poland.

A multitude of thoughts passed through my head, all at the same time. "Oh, Shit!" being the first word that came to mind. And then I realized - no one knows where I am! I don't even know where I am. I am going to miss meeting my mom in Poland. I wonder what a Belarus prison is like. This is probably the one place where being an "American" is not going to help me. I knew next to nothing about Belarus. Was it still a communist country? Did they know that the Soviet Union had broken up? I had absolutely no idea. I had this unspoken feeling that Belarus wasn't going to roll out the red carpet for a young American girl passing through. I somehow managed to stand next to the tattooed guard and not fall to the ground, curl up in a ball, suck my thumb and start muttering to myself, "I'm an American, I'm an American."

The guard says something to the ladies in my compartment and motions towards me to follow him with his dollar sign tattooed digit. Shaking and trying to stay composed, I follow him down the corridor of the train car. We get to the exit door of the train car, and I am jerked off balance as the train starts to move. The guard jumps off the last stair of the train onto the platform as the train is moving and wants me to follow. "What kind of hell is this!" I said to no one in particular, or maybe I screamed it in my head. I had no choice but to jump off the train too. This was it. I was going to a *gulag*, never to be heard from again.

Somehow, I landed on my feet as the train continued down the tracks. The platform was directly in front of the train station. It was quiet, lit with a few streetlights, and had a few men in uniform milling around. I looked around, considering my options. It wasn't like one of those fugitive movies where I could duck down into a crowd of travelers or make a break for the Belorussian forest. I didn't think I would get far with guard dogs nipping at my heels. I was alone. Resigned to my fate, I followed the guard inside the station. Entering the building, I knew I had no hope of getting out of there unscathed. I had no idea what was going to happen. Any color on my cheeks from the crisp night air was completely drained from my face. Bewildered and scared, I stood in the main part of the station. To my right was a row of what looked like ticket booths. I was in the middle of the huge building with a closed, dark kiosk on my left and another train platform straight ahead. The guard with the dollar sign tattoo told me to wait where we stood, in the middle of the station. Stark white floors and walls and harsh fluorescent overhead lights surrounded me and did little to ease my anxiety. The place was quiet despite guards walking around, the quiet that comes at three in the morning. I took the guard's words literally and stood glued to the exact spot where he had left me.

After a few minutes, the guard came back with another guy in uniform. This new guy had more epaulets on his shoulder and a peaked military cap. This was the "big" guy, or should I say the little guy. This officer was a thin 5 foot 7. Both guards stand in front of me as the officer flips through my passport again as if a visa for Belarus was going to magically appear in my passport. The officer starts asking questions right out of a stereotypical Cold War movie.

- "Where are you going?"
- "Who are you meeting?"
- "What is your purpose?" - (Really?!)

Was this really how it worked? Ferreting out spies crossing the border by asking these standard questions hoping the suspected spy will break under questioning and spill all their secrets. Was it now my turn to start demanding to speak to someone from the U.S. Embassy, or does that come later?

I answer the questions as the officer continues to flip through my passport while simultaneously trying to tilt his head back and look down his nose at me. Since I was taller than him, this was a ridiculous move. It's then that I realize a girl shaking in her boots was the only tactic to take in this situation. From his attempt at an air of superiority, it was clear that I was supposed to be the docile woman cowering in the face of authority.

Luckily, I was already shaking. Slouching my shoulders and looking down at the ground, I answered the officer's questions.

Eventually, after what felt like hours, the questions were answered to their satisfaction, and the two men conferred with each other a few steps away. It took the two surprisingly little time to decide my fate. The guard with the dollar sign tattoo led me to the small kiosk with a big window and curtain that was on the side of the room, near where I was questioned. I was a little confused as the curtain was drawn across the window, and the inside of the kiosk was dark. The guard again told me to stand in front of the window and wait as he walked away. Five minutes went by as I pondered what the heck was happening. The train, with my big backpack still on board, had already left the station. It was the middle of the night. No one knew where I was, including me. And yet, here I was, standing in front of an obviously empty wooden kiosk somewhere in Belarus.

Suddenly with an unexpected flourish, the curtains were whipped open inside the kiosk, and the light switched on, which was weird because no one had entered the kiosk. There, on the other side of the glass, was an older, round, stereotypical soviet woman staring at me with a less than happy expression. Probably because I had woken her up in the middle of the night. The old woman shoved a form under the glass, and I began filling it out as best I could. I was like a 5-year-old sounding out words. The form was in Russian. Even if it was written in Ukrainian, I would still be clueless. Luckily, the dollar sign tattoo guy came back to check on me and help me fill out the form. Forty U.S. dollars later, I had a fresh visa in my passport that would allow me to ride the train through Belarus on my way to Poland. My train had already left the station, so not sure why I needed the visa.

Still a little bewildered by what was happening, the dollar sign tattoo guy told me to wait in the middle of the cavernous building again. I wondered what else could happen to me. Not knowing what was going to happen, I waited and paced back and forth the same 10 feet of the floor. Back and forth. Back and forth. Scared out of my mind, until the same guard came back again. I was beginning to think of him as a friend even though I didn't know his name and never thought to ask. Was he my handler now? How did this work exactly? Was I going straight to the *gulag* or another round of interrogation, maybe in a room with a one-way window and a bright light in my face? Instead, he escorted me to the train platform on the other side of the station, and we waited again. There was a train sitting on the tracks, and it started to leave when we stepped onto the platform. Not knowing what was going on, I figured, ok my backpack was probably already in Poland, and my things were being distributed among the conductors on the train. I wondered how much American jeans and t-shirts were going for on the open market? The real question was, where are they going to take me? Was I going to leave this place? Or were they getting ready to transport me to the nearest facility for unwanted foreigners that accidentally wandered over the Belorussian border?

After what seemed like hours, another train pulls up. The guard tells me to get on, and to my astonishment, it is my original train. A look back at my friend/handler, and he was already headed back into the station. No goodbye, no wave of his tattooed hand, nothing. Typical. You form a meaningful connection with a handsome border guard, and he doesn't even say goodbye. Well, I didn't like you all that much anyway, Boris or whatever your name was. Hmmph. I wonder if he ever thinks of me.

I return to the same compartment; the Ukrainian ladies are still there, and amazingly, so is my backpack. I was totally confused until I realized that this border was the same as the Polish border. While I was getting my $40 visa, the train was driven off to change its wheels and return to the station. Seriously, they lift each train car, take the wheels off and put new ones on. This whole process was left over from World War II when the train tracks in the U.S.S.R were built narrower to delay enemy trains from easily crossing over borders.

I melted into my train bed, relieved to have the ordeal behind me. I continued uneventfully to Warsaw. I was meeting my mother in the lobby of a *Holiday Inn* near the train station. I realized when I entered Poland that I was arriving in Warsaw at 8 a.m. and my mother wasn't arriving until 4 p.m. I was exhausted from my ordeal, and I did not want to drag my big bag around Warsaw. I headed to the hotel and chose a nice comfortable chair in the lobby facing a huge wall of windows. Alternating sleeping and reading, I spent the whole day waiting in the hotel lobby. Finally, my mom showed up at the hotel. I was so happy to have someone from home. We left Warsaw the next day and headed for Kracow. Traveling around a bit, we went from Kracow to Budapest by train. I missed American restaurants so much that I made my mom go to every chain restaurant that we came across.

In the past, my mother had traveled in Western Europe a bit but had never been to Eastern Europe. She was a trooper as we explored Kracow and Budapest, then took a train heading to Ukraine. The long hours on the train and the inconvenience of travel in Ukraine were a shock to my mother, but we made it to Nizhyn. We spent a few days resting in Nizhyn and had a day trip to Kiev. Soon, it was time to head home, and I was on the same flight as my mom, heading back to Wisconsin. I was so excited to be going home for a break. At passport control and customs in Chicago, I had one of those "Did I say that out loud moments."

Waiting in the long lines, I said to my mother, "I bet they even speak English." The guy ahead of us in line looked back with a look that said, "What is wrong with that chick?" Can't blame him. The ramblings of a chick that has been living in Ukraine for too long never make sense.

CHAPTER 18
DUH! HE IS JUST NOT THAT IN TO YOU

I went home for a visit between my first and second years. Yeah, it's not recommended, and depending on where you go in the Peace Corps, it is time and cost-prohibitive. In my defense, or should I say my pathetic excuse, Jen, my roommate, had left. I was homesick and really couldn't face another year in Ukraine without going home for a respite from the trials and tribulations of my life in Ukraine. I needed to hear English spoken by the general public. I wanted *Doritos* and peanut butter *M&M's*. I wanted to go into a grocery store and see long aisles filled with the products I had been dreaming about. I bought a ticket home, intending to take full advantage of life in America. Some volunteers took the opportunity to travel during this time, a few put together a kid's English summer camp, and a bunch of people had already left Ukraine for good. The Institute was closed for the summer. No students and very little, if any, staff. If I had stayed, it would have been a very long summer of absolutely nothing to do.

I loved being back in my hometown. The warm summer nights were what I missed. The town festivals, 4th of July, softball games, and shopping in stores that had everything I wanted and missed. I was pretty excited to be back in the U.S. I immediately fell completely and totally in love. The kind of love that makes people break into spontaneous songs for no reason, with rainbows, sunshine, and songbirds bringing your hair ribbon and a robe in the morning. It was a bit of a love triangle. I just couldn't decide which I loved more- the washer or the dryer. Those clean white metal machines with their wonderful buttons. Wash, rinse, spin, dry- oh my- it was all so wonderful, and they made me so happy. I would sometimes pass by, reach my hand out to touch the cool white metal, and softly whisper, "We will meet again soon, my love." No pounding clothes in a basin with cold water, no trying to wring jeans out and failing miserably, so that a long stream of water ran down the hallway from the clothesline where the jeans were hung. Yep, I was blissfully in a *ménage à trois*, and I didn't care who knew it.

Falling into old habits quickly, I went to a softball game that the old neighborhood boys were playing. The whole gang was there, including "Jake." Sigh. I had a lot of time over the course of the year to think about Jake. We had exchanged a couple of letters, and I was as confused as ever. Too much time on my hands led to analyzing his letters and hours spent crafting a response letter with just the right balance of questions for him to respond to, interesting stories, funny anecdotes, and a hint of sexual innuendo. All my creative energy was spent on those letters, carefully tailoring them with what I thought would pique Jake's interest, which also included a couple of cringe-worthy, suggestive poems that I had hoped would add a little intrigue. Poems that have long since been tossed in the trash. Right, Jake, she asked hopefully? I also spent time thinking about what I would say to Jake when we saw each other again.

It was like time had stood still. The same softball game, the same beer at the local bar, the same people, and the same unreciprocated crush. The topic of conversation with the neighborhood boys was still the Green Bay Packers, for the most part. However, there were new things to catch up on. One of the brothers had gotten engaged, and there were one or two new faces on the softball team.

That first night, to my surprise, "Jake" offered to give me a ride home at the end of the night when I mentioned I didn't have a car. This was a landmark offer that had no precedence. Most of the time I spent around Jake, I had a car, but it was also subtly implied that he wasn't interested in giving me a ride home or spending time with me alone in general.

The windows were down in Jake's late model, gray station wagon, and I commented on how much I missed the warm Monona nights. My hand sticking out the car window, carried by the wind, I was feeling excited and happy. The ride was quiet with the radio on, and I was relishing every second of the summer breeze and sitting next to Jake. I am not sure why I was so attracted to Jake. He rarely gave me the time of day. We would chat at the bar after softball games. The occasional mutual attraction had in the past led to him giving me a mixed tape that he had been listening to in his car and some hugging in the parking lot, and once or twice an invitation to go ice skating, with a bunch of his brothers, of course. Our occasional letter correspondence only added fuel to my already confused mind. Did he like me or not? I would have had better luck figuring that out if I picked the petals off a flower. His letters were barely decipherable scribbles with newsy tidbits on how the *Green Bay Packers* were doing and what the family was up to, dotted with nuggets of "You are missed" and signed, "Love, Jake." The letters alone were enough to send a lonely girl starved for affection into an overheated frenzy of confusion and angst.

During the car ride home, I contemplated if it would be weird if I just threw myself over the stick shift and attacked him like a soldier that had come home from war. I had so much pent-up energy and need for close human contact that I was willing to throw caution to the wind and go for it. I had it all planned out. I was going with the direct approach. I had always thought of Jake as a "tell it like it is kind of guy," so that was what I was going to do. No messing around with innuendo and subtle hints of what I wanted. I wanted Jake in the worst way and was going to point-blank tell him that. I wanted a wild and crazy summer with as much fun as I could fit in, and Jake was welcome to come along for the ride. A summer fling was on my mind.

The trouble was I had never in my life done something even remotely like the scenario I had written in my head. The reality that night was more like: quiet, quiet, "Ahh, I brought you something.. Ah, um.. I have a lot of people that I thought were friends that never wrote to me. So... (awkward pause again)... Thank you," as I handed over the bottle of vodka I had brought back for him. Then came the long awkward silence as I slowly moved my hand to the car door and got out. Neither one of us said anything for what felt like an hour. Stunned by my own ineptness, I dragged my feet to the front door of my house, opened the front door, walked in, and quickly shut it behind me as I broke into a fit of flailing arms and legs stomping the ground like a madwoman, frustrated with my awkward self. Errrrr. It was going to be a lonely summer.

My time home that summer continued much the same. I often volunteered to go to the grocery store just so I could linger down the aisles. Somehow, life had gone on while I was away. I had lots of free time. Friends and family were working during the day, and some friends had moved away. One of my sisters got married during this time. I went stag to the wedding, not by choice, more like absolutely no date prospects. The bartender for the wedding reception was a high school friend of my brother and a friend of the family. We had flirted occasionally, but it was another one of those one-sided relationships that I was increasingly afraid was going to become the only type of interactions I was going to have with the opposite sex.

Anyway, toward the end of the night, he abandoned his post behind the bar and asked me to dance the last slow dance of the night. It would have been perfect if he hadn't uttered those six words that quickly dissolved all hope - "Kathy, you are Brian's little sister." Wow, didn't see that one coming, and what does that mean anyway? Or maybe he was just trying to distance himself from the sight of my unfortunate wedding hair, an almost exact replica of Loretta Lynn on stage singing *Coal Miner's Daughter*. I may never know the true reason for his brush off.

I had not lost complete hope for my envisioned wild summer because one of the new guys on the softball team hit on me. He was always making everyone laugh with his jokes, quick wit, and voice impressions. A boyish charm with curly hair and exuded a sincerity by looking you in the eyes when he talked to you. I liked him but didn't know too much about him. We wildly flirted at the local festival, and with the help of alcohol, the great fear eraser, I invited him to watch the 4th of July fireworks the next night. I dressed in my best "going to the beer tent" outfit with the usual mood ring accessory (hey, it was a conversation piece) and a low-cut shirt and high-cut shorts. As the sun went down, I made my way to the festival grounds. We were supposed to meet at the beer tent. I got there, and a few of the softball brothers were there, including Jake. I waited with them, constantly looking around until one of the brothers told me that the "new guy" wasn't coming and apologized on his behalf. Disappointed, I stood and watched the fireworks next to Jake and the others, wondering if the summer was going to be a total bust. Wanting nothing more than to buy Jake a beer and ask, "Do I have some kind of don't ask me out stamp on my forehead?" that says, "don't ask this chick out, and if you do, don't bother showing up." That didn't happen. I walked home alone that night, questions not asked.

A few days later, I went to downtown Madison to do a little shopping. I knew the "New Guy" worked in the skilled trades somewhere on the university campus, and I was hoping to accidentally run into him on his lunch break. I had already practiced my "Wow, what a surprise to run into you" look. I also hoped I hadn't crossed the line into stalker territory. It was a long shot, but amazingly, we ran into each other right in front of the campus bookstore. Both of us with big goofy smiles on our faces. He was with his co-workers but stopped in front of me as his co-workers kept walking. We exchanged greetings, and almost immediately, he asked me to a movie for the following night. Forgetting about being stood up on the 4th of July, I immediately accepted. He said he still had my phone number, which I had cleverly written on Ukrainian paper money a week before. We said goodbye and continued on our way. Wow, finally I had a date. I was excited, to say the least.

The next day, I took my time getting ready. Had the perfect outfit picked out. A cobalt blue t-shirt and matching skirt combo. I took extra time to do my hair, and I waited. We hadn't set an exact time. I assumed that he would call me to set the time of our date. I waited some more. Staying close to the phone and ready to jump on it. I continued to wait and wait. At about 6 p.m., I was starting to question myself. Did I get something wrong? Did he ask me out? I worked up the courage to give him a call, using my mom's landline telephone. Ah, the ancient times before cell phones when you could make an anonymous phone call. Even though caller ID wasn't a common thing yet, I am 100% sure the other end of that phone line knew exactly who was calling. Calming my nervousness and breathing deeply, I slowly dialed the number and hung up quickly before finishing. Ugh. Why did I have to call? What was happening? Again, I screwed up my courage this time. I dialed all the numbers and put the receiver to my ear. A man answered, not the new guy, with what sounded like a small party going on in the background. I lost my nerve again and quickly hung up without saying a word. What the hell was wrong with me? Dial the number, listen to the ringing, and speak when the ringing stops. A simple concept that was somehow beyond my grasp.

Still walking around the house in my bathrobe, not wanting to get my "going out clothes" sweaty, I paced around and waited about a half-hour and gathered what little courage I had and dialed again. This time, an abrasive woman yelled into the phone. Stunned to have a woman answer, I stood speechless with the phone to my ear. It felt like I stood frozen for 20 minutes, but it was probably like 30 seconds before I wordlessly hung up the phone again. And simultaneously put my fingers in an L-shape on my forehead. Well, that was smooth. So much for my Saturday date night, instead a lonely evening at home watching tv. Gee, so glad I flew half-way around the world to subject myself to this humiliation.

The New Guy did reluctantly offer a reason for standing me up after the next softball game. At the after-game gathering, at the local bar/bowling alley, sitting at the bar avoiding looking me in the eyes, he reluctantly spits out that he had a girlfriend and that is why he didn't go through with the date. I sat on my barstool, looking around the bar at the rest of the people, seeing if anyone else was noticing my humiliation. Luckily, everyone else seemed to be in small groups of their own. At least that was the impression I had, but I had no doubt this interaction was a topic of conversation among the other patrons/the rest of the softball team/neighborhood boys. It may have been a group of mostly men, but they gossiped like a bunch of pre-teens in middle school. As I scanned the room, my eyes came to a stop on Jake. Sitting alone on the other side of the bar, drinking a beer. Sigh. Once again, the road led back to Jake. Cue every '80s romance movie montage sequence that has ever been made. The smiles, the conversations, ice skating, the letters, was it meaningless to him? The New Guy had stopped talking as I slipped off my barstool. I patted his shoulder and said, "Thanks for wasting my time," resisting the urge to add the word "asshole." I was a lady, after all.

I sat down next to Jake and poured myself more beer from the team pitcher sitting on the bar. I thought about asking him why he never asked me out but didn't have enough liquid courage for that. We sat chatting and drinking until I looked around and noticed that everyone else on the team had left the bar. Already on the tipsy side, I said out loud that I would probably have to walk home tonight. He must have also been in a good mood, after a couple of beers, and offered to give me a ride home. Upon arrival at home, we promptly started making out in his car like a couple of drunk teenagers, only stopping when Jake saw that my sister was looking out the front door window to see what the dog was barking at. I reminded Jake that I was only home for a little while longer, hoping he would take the hint and we would spend some time together before I went back to Ukraine. Leaning against the passenger side door, I reached behind me and opened the door, almost rolling out of the car backward. Classy move, I know.

I never received a call from Jake. In the history of the cliche, "He's just not that into you" it was never more applicable than this time in my life. If that wasn't enough, the night before I headed back to Ukraine, I was at a post softball tournament party. The whole team and their respective partners were there celebrating the team's win at the tournament. It was a subdued night since it was a Sunday. People watching tv or hanging out on the back porch. The New Guy was there, alone, but left early. As he was leaving, he stopped in front of me, took my hand in both his hands, looked me in the eye, and said he was happy to meet me and wished me well. Not sure if he did this because I was leaving the next day or if that night was the last softball game of the year. Either way, I muttered "sure" and stopped myself from asking if his girlfriend was wondering where he was.

Later, Jake announced his departure to the group as a whole. Never saying goodbye to me or even looking in my direction. He knew, or maybe most likely didn't remember, that I was leaving the next day. My staring directly at him with a look of astonishment on my face that he wasn't going to say goodbye had no effect on him. I was disheartened and dejected. Another lonely drive home for me that night. That was the defining moment for me. I knew this crush, or whatever you want to call it, had to be over.

CHAPTER 19

BACK AGAIN, BUT SUMMER ISN'T OVER

I checked in for my flight back to Ukraine with bags so heavy I could only drag them across the airport floor to the check-in counter. This time, I had packed a little better with plenty of things I needed and missed. I even had some room for *Diet Dr. Pepper* for Opal, my new roommate, in my bag. Packed on a Polish airline with a bunch of kids from Belarus returning from a sponsored trip to the States, I had several hours on the plane to think about my time at home and also develop a new mantra. Instead of "I don't have anything else to do" that I had been repeating on a regular basis for a year, my new mantra was, "It is time to move on." I wasn't going to waste more time hoping Jake would suddenly wake up and want to spend time with me. I was saying goodbye to not only the thought of Jake but to the small-town life that was all I knew. Yes, I had a great time at home, but everyone had moved on with their lives. Was it me that was different, or was it them? I don't know, but what I did know was that it was time to fully embrace a different life. Home was always going to be home, but I had joined the Peace Corps for a reason. I couldn't take the road less traveled if I had one foot on the path to home.

The flight was uneventful, and I had made arrangements with Oleksandr, my coordinator, to have a car and driver pick me up at the airport and drive me back to Nizhyn. Opal came with the driver as she was going crazy with being by herself all those weeks. About half-way through the drive back, a small stone flew up and hit the windshield, completely shattering it. A spiderweb of crackling glass filled the entire windshield to the point where the driver had to stick his head out the side window for the rest of the drive. An appropriate welcome back to Ukraine, if there ever was one. This was the start of year two in Ukraine. I had lived in Ukraine for a year, and I had a better sense of how things worked. I also knew that the non-sensical life that is Ukraine would bring all new frustrations, laughter, and adventures. I was ready, I thought.

Tentative plans had been made before I went to the States for a trip to Estonia with Kathleen, Marie, and Opal. After a few days of hot weather and nothing-to-do boredom, those tentative plans became concrete. We agreed to meet in Kiev to begin the adventure. First, a train to Krakow, then Warsaw, then to Gdansk, Poland, where we would take a special train to Tallinn, Estonia. An uneventful trip in the beginning. We had lived in a former Soviet Republic for a year, yet we were still delusional enough to think that travel would be easy.

In Gdansk, we made the excruciating long trek to find a dormitory that we had read about in *Let's Go Europe*. Walking single file down a busy road in the hot sun with heavy backpacks and diminishing enthusiasm, only to find the first well-hidden hostel was full. Eventually, with a lot of hand gestures and asking around, we found another dormitory. It was similar to the dorm in Nizhyn. Four rooms attached by a short hallway and a shared shower/toilet. Opal did her usual shower at night and sleeping in the clothes she was going to wear the next day. A quirk revealed on this trip. In the morning, she popped up, ready to go.

We had bought tickets on a special train that went up the coast through Lithuania, Latvia, and to the last stop of Tallinn, Estonia. At the train station, we discovered a train that stood out with its distinctive purple and pink colors waiting at the station. Marie and Opal started to feel sick fairly quickly after we boarded this fancy train. If I had to guess, it was the questionable-looking sandwiches with little gnats flying around the glass display case at the train station that they bought for the train ride. I, on the other hand, was in air-conditioned heaven riding a clean, nice train, and I was just enjoying the ride, happy that I had stuck to factory packaged chips and chocolate for my train snack.

In the middle of the night, as, again, these types of things always happen, we crossed the border into Latvia. What should have been a routine border crossing went crazy in a very short amount of time. As armed guards with security dogs rushed about checking for contraband (vodka and cigarettes), the passport control guards arrived at our compartment and asked for our passports. We sleepily handed them over. We just wanted to go back to sleep. As the guards went through our passports page by page, they began talking between themselves in the hallway.

Flipping through the passports one final time with serious looks on their faces, they uttered the words that would change the mood and course of the entire trip: "You have no visa, you have to get off the train. Gather your bags and come with me," said one of the guards in broken English. We tried to argue, "But we were told you don't need a visa." The guard was not persuaded by our words of reason and common sense. We hurriedly gathered our bags and, in a single file line, followed the guard off the train. Passing another compartment with Americans in their 60s, we hear them arguing with the guard about the same visa situation we had. Somehow, I think the guards gave up because we didn't see those people at the train station. More than likely, the older tourists folded a few American dollars into their passports to facilitate the visa process without leaving the train. Two young college-age guys joined us at the train station. College fraternity types that were half awake and resigned to our same fate. We were told to wait at the train station, and not a word was said of our fate, stuck in the middle of nowhere. And wait, we did. It was 4 o'clock in the morning in a quiet, dark train station. The only sound was the hustle and bustle of the guards as they finished their search of the train. This whole scenario was becoming sadly familiar. Never did I think that the sights and sounds of armed guards leading me off trains in the middle of the night would become a reoccurring theme in my life. We are talking about a girl whose most daring escapade growing up was sneaking over to the park across the street with the neighborhood kids after curfew while our parents sat around the neighbor's fire pit, oblivious to where we were. Or the time in high school when my friends and I passed around a bottle of wine, in a parked car, before going to the high school dance. I guess, if I think about it, being escorted off of a train, not once, but twice by armed foreign government soldiers, was just par for the course for this rebel.

After waiting for a few hours, we were herded onto the back of a military truck, and as the sun came up, we rode the bumpy road back to the Latvian border. There we would wait again. Sitting on the floor of the military border building making small talk with the frat boy college students while the guards filled out their paperwork. We still didn't get what was going on. None of the guards talked to us; we were just sitting at the guard station waiting.

Finally, we were told we could go and that there was a bus that would take us to the border- again. Somehow, we managed to buy tickets and cram ourselves in the last few seats on the bus to the Latvian border. Our nice, air-conditioned purple and pink train was long gone, and we were out a ride to Estonia and the money we had already paid for the "special train." Marie was still sick and throwing up into a *ziplock* as the bus rolled down the road. Opal wasn't hailing much better but managed to survive the bus ride. Before long, we stopped AGAIN at the border and had to get off the bus to get a Latvian visa. The sticking point was that the Latvian visa was free, but we needed that free sticker visa in our passports before trying to cross a border. We watched the border guards put the free Latvian visa sticker in our passports with dejection and disbelief. We silently filed back on the bus and rode the rest of the way to Riga, the capital city of Latvia.

Riga was the epitome of Soviet architecture and despair, at least the area near the train station was. It matched our mood. We didn't want to wander around as we were hoping to leave Riga and Latvia as fast as we could. Somehow, we found a hostel across the street from the train station and booked two rooms. Afterward, we made our way back to the train station to ask about train tickets so we could continue our journey. Unbelievably there were tickets available for later that same night. It wasn't the same special purple and pink train, but we took what we could get. We used our rooms to shower and relax for a little bit before the train. The woman at the front desk of the hostel was very confused that we only used the room for a couple of hours, but we were hell-bent on getting out of Latvia as soon as possible.

Tallinn was beautiful, bright, and a breath of fresh air. The cobblestone streets of the city center and the dragon-shaped water spouts hanging off the old church in the main square were therapeutic to help forget our recent travel problems. We wandered the sights and sounds of the city for a few days. Browsed bookstores with books in English and local outdoor markets, where I bought a handmade wool sweater with a delicate floral design. The concrete soviet apartment monstrosities were conveniently on the outskirts of the city, mostly out of sight when you were in the town center. Unfortunately, time passed quickly, and soon, it was time to think about the trip back. Staring at the map at a local travel agency, we contemplated our options. Kathleen and Marie were continuing their trip in a more circular route. They were going to Russia. The visa rules for Americans in Russian were tough and impossible to navigate on your own. They were working with a travel agency for train tickets and a place to stay.

Opal and I, however, were backtracking the way we came. We had a couple of options. First up, a train from Estonia directly to Kiev. I nixed this idea right away because the train route went through Belarus. No way in hell was I doing that again. I got anxious just by the suggestion of a train anywhere near Belarus. The others didn't understand my reluctance; no, that is not the right word. My downright adamant "no" to getting on a train that, according to the map, clearly goes through Belarus. Since Opal wasn't going to travel back to Ukraine by herself, she had to go the way

I was going. The only option was a train from Tallinn to Warsaw, then Warsaw to Krakow, then finally, Krakow to Kiev. It was an exhausting trip. Hours and hours on trains. Reading, sleeping, and endless hours to think about the upcoming year, my lack of love life, and what I wanted to do with my life. At least I had another story to write to people back home.

CHAPTER 20
YEAR TWO, HERE WE GO AGAIN

The sun rose over the horizon, revealing a golden glow that surrounded the trees like a halo of polished perfection. The sounds of the morning were a symphony as the birds sang their melodious, cheery songs, and the blowing breeze softly rustled the grass and gently woke me from my slumber. Outside my front door, the vivid greens of the foliage unfolded before me, and the indigo hues of the open sky went on for miles and miles. This unique blend of sights and sounds enticing me towards a day close to perfection. Poof! The reality was drastically different. If you have read my ramblings up until this point, you would know that wasn't me. My story could never start with such poetic descriptions by a starry-eyed volunteer out to save the world. Sure, those volunteers exist, at least I hope they do. I would hate to think this volunteer is only a myth.

The reality of my life in Ukraine was a little more subdued. I was awakened by the rumblings of diesel trucks outside my window. Then wrestling the five wool blankets off my bed, I grudgingly crawled from my bed, wearing two layers of pajamas, and stumbled to the shower where I discovered that no water was coming out of the faucet. In the kitchen, I find nothing but stale bread and bottled water, necessitating yet another fruitless trip to see if there was anything to buy on the shelves of the stores.

Unfazed and resigned to another obstacle-filled day, I dressed in several layers and put on my triple goose down coat, and stepped outside to be slapped in the face by the bitter cold and austere buildings of a crumbling economy. Lines at the bread store, bare shelves in stores, a broken transportation system, and poverty were a part of my current life and had become the norm.

The challenge in year two of living in Ukraine was the knowledge of how things work but also knowing that it didn't matter. Sure, the taxi driver, there were only a handful in town, knew where the Americans lived and would drive us home from the train station without us having to say a word. And yes, I knew I had to buy envelopes and stamps for my letters home, at the post office. Unfortunately, that knowledge was useless and incredibly frustrating when, for weeks, the ladies in the post office continued to tell me they were out of envelopes. The positives and negatives of my life in Ukraine were a delicate balance that could go either way at any moment. However, it did push me to be more creative. Did you know that by tearing out pages from my Peace Corps medical manual, I could repurpose them into envelopes? The chances of my needing to know the symptoms of Malaria were slim anyway.

I wouldn't say excitement was the best word to describe my feelings about starting year two in Ukraine. More like bland resignation. I was back in Ukraine, might as well get on with it. The school year started much the same as the year before. Waiting around until classes started. Spending my time washing clothes, shopping for food, writing letters home. I also restarted going to a nearby stadium with a running track. I started to become a little obsessive about going to the track every day. It helped clear my head. I would just walk around the oval track, but something about the repetitiveness was helpful. Every once in a while, something interesting would happen. Like when people would come through and walk straight across the middle of the walled stadium and then disappear. It was so weird. I would see little old ladies walk with bags in their hands, then suddenly, they were gone. It took longer than I want to admit to realize that there were a couple of hay bales stacked up along the lower wall in the back corner of the stadium to assist with the disappearing act. Mystery solved.

Then there was the time a drunk man had passed out and was sleeping in the bleachers. As I walked around my circle, I watched a couple of kids sneak up to the sleeping, disheveled old man and as slowly as they could reach around the guy to grab all the empty beer bottles lying around him so they could take the empties to the store to collect the deposit. Most mornings, I was alone as I walked. I thought I was just quietly doing my thing until one of my students, Max, asked in class if I "went in for sport." Gasp! The American was walking at the track. One of the tamer gossip pieces that would mark year two of my stint.

Like the first year, Oleksander kept telling us that classes would start next week, then the next week. I had ample time to get my lesson plans all prepared. M. Somerset Maugham's book, *Theatre*, was on the class reading list this year. This book was typical of the school's British English coursework with textbooks from the 1950s. British English was taught at the Institute, or I should say British English from 1952. I am sure it was a shock to everyone to hear a native English speaker, especially like myself, speaking English they had only heard in American movies. A curriculum based on memorization and recitation required certain route phrases and pronunciations that I found amusing. Young school children seeing my roommate and I out in public would shout the only words they knew, which were also the words to their memorized dialogues that started with the words, "my working day..." then go on to describe how they woke up and went to school.

When I assigned my students a creative essay assignment, so many students used the phrases "cozy like nook" and "to my mind" to start a paragraph. I almost thought they had all copied the same essay, but then I realized those were the memorized phrases that all the students used in their other classes. This was better than the youth in the general public yelling variations of "fuck" because that was the only word they knew based on the American movies they had seen. A fellow volunteer was once stopped while walking down the street to answer questions on how to conjugate the word fuck. I also had a group of male students ask me about American swear words. Feeling a little daring, one day towards the end of my second year, I held a short, impromptu tutoring session after class on swear words, forms, and phrases. Providing a well-rounded education and expansive vocabulary was part of the job, right? Well, I figured it couldn't hurt to encourage educational inquisitiveness. I also tried to slip in a benign word and try to pass it off as a swear word, just for fun. I don't think the students believed me. I don't know what the "bucky" was wrong with them?

Opal was clueless as far as cooking, so I took over a lot of things. Making meatballs for her involved placing balls of ground beef on a tray for the oven. No seasoning, no breadcrumbs nothing. Even me, with my limited repertoire of recipes, knew that wasn't quite right. We didn't go over to the little back room of the defunct cafeteria for meals at all. Grilled cheese with sausage sandwiches was again the house specialty after some discussion of the correct way to butter the bread for the sandwiches. The great grilled cheese debate, maybe you have heard of it? Did you butter the outside of the bread slice only, the outside and inside of the bread slice, or put butter in the pan and not spread it on the bread itself? I was a butter the inside and outside bread person, and Opal was a butter in the pan person. Maybe that was a clue to future incompatibility? Opal and I also spent a lot of time playing cards and *Scrabble* in the evenings. Hours and hours of nothing to do.

When we finally had access to the previously locked fourth room in our suite of dorm rooms, Opal moved into it. It was a much larger room. I was fine in my room stuffed with a huge wardrobe, a desk, and a twin bed. The room that my previous roommate, Jen, had used became the library. The cupboard in that room held all the donations and books we had picked up in the Peace Corps office and during our travels. It also included all the magazines that had been sent to us. I was reading my way through the shelves. From classics like Steinbeck to the mysteries of Mary Higgins-Clark, I read them all.

Early in the semester, a few of Opal's students invited us to visit their home city. It was about an hour and a half away by electric train. I am not sure why I went, but like most things, I didn't have anything else to do. This new city, Chernigov, was where many students at the Institute called home. Luckily, one of our student hosts had an apartment that Opal and I could stay in for the weekend by ourselves. Thus, started the food coma weekend. Just a non-stop gluttony of food. Every time we turned around, students were bringing food to the apartment we were staying in, or we were going to another student's family house for a meal. At one point, I found myself sitting at a table with a student's mother on one side of me and the grandmother on the other side. This is the absolute worst meal scenario that you can get in Ukraine. To top it off, it was mushroom picking season. Every surface of the family's kitchen was covered with baskets and bowls of mushrooms. So many mushrooms.

Back to the scenario that you don't want to find yourself in as a guest at someone's house in Ukraine. "What's the big deal?" You may be asking yourself. Well, let me tell you. I had both the mother and grandmother putting food on my plate and telling me I had to try the many, many varieties of mushrooms that they had. "Oh, try this one, and this one, it's very good."

It was impossible to say "no" to having more food put on your plate. It's rude to refuse more food in Ukraine; otherwise, the mother and/or grandmother start asking if you don't like their food and often go on to lament to those around them, and possibly the neighbors next door, that the Americans don't like their food. Added to this problematic situation was the fact we were told, by the Peace Corps staff not to eat mushrooms or wild game because of the effect Chernobyl had on nature. I caved that night and had some mushrooms. It was all delicious but only added to my gastronomic misery. The golden lesson learned from this that I now pass on to you, my friend, is never, ever clean your plate when having a meal as a guest in someone's home in Ukraine. Always leave a little something on the plate; otherwise, the host will add more to your plate despite your protests. Instead, put a little food on your plate, making sure to try everything on the table, then while eating, make the appropriate "yummy" sounds and express words of how good everything tastes. Then leave a little food on your plate. Simple, yet effective. You are welcome.

I realize that until this point, I have never mentioned one of the worst disasters affecting many parts of Europe, but mainly associated with Ukraine, Chernobyl. I mention it now because the city we were in, Chernigov, was only about fifty miles or so from the city that was the site of the reactors. Chernobyl had happened a mere eight years before we arrived in Ukraine. It was a talked about topic and many people, including my students, had personal stories.

One student told of being sent to what authorities called a summer camp in the Republic of Georgia after the nuclear accident. The student was traumatized by being separated from her parents at a young age and sent to a completely different country. The student also shared how the food was meager and that packages and money sent by parents to their children at camp were often not given to the children. Rather, they were kept by the adults tasked with taking care of the children. What some people don't know about the Chernobyl disaster is that because of the way the winds were blowing that day, the radiation was blown more towards northern Ukraine and into Belarus. Also not widely publicized was that many people in Ukraine were not told about the radiation leak for many days. There was propaganda and a cover-up of information. The topic of Chernobyl is a big one, and I could go on and on about it. However, I will leave the matter up to the experts. Books have been written, and movies have been made that do a much better job covering the topic than I ever could.

Back in the dorm after our little weekend adventure, things were the same. Not surprisingly, my second year in Ukraine had started with little difference from the first year. Like most days, I was decked in my usual "not going to leave my room" dormitory attire, light blue sweatpants about two sizes too big, rolled at the waist, my *Tigger* sleeping t-shirt that hung down to my knees with a light blue XL sweatshirt over it. Socks and slippers completed the ensemble. It was the attire of the lazy with no place to go and nothing to do.

As I was puttering around my room, there was a knock at the door. My room was the closest to our main door, so I was usually the first to answer. Opal didn't come out of her room. Thinking it was one of the dorm monitor ladies from down the hall, I was surprised to see this tall, young guy standing in the doorway. Dressed in jeans, a green plaid shirt, and a backpack slung over his shoulder. He didn't have the usual crew cut or shaved head of the other male students at the Institute. Instead, the sides and back of his head were shaved, but the top was left long with gelled corkscrew tendrils falling haphazardly around. It gave him a more European look and was different than the other guys I had seen in Ukraine. In heavily accented English, the guy at the door asked if he could borrow a book. We, Opal and I, had put the word out that we had books and that students were free to borrow them. We didn't want to put them in a room at the Institute yet, because we were afraid the teachers and admin wouldn't let students borrow the books. Only a couple of students took us up on the offer of borrowing our books.

The student at the door followed me to the book room, and I opened the cupboard, revealing our inventory. After a quick glance, he asked, "Which book was good for a boy?" Smiling, I pointed him towards the John Grisham books while at the same time thinking to myself- I don't think "boy" is an accurate description. He was slightly taller than me, lean, attractive, and most definitely not a "boy."

After selecting a book for "Curly Boy," as he was now dubbed, I walked him back to the door. Leaning against the closed door after he left, I let out a sigh and went to tell Opal about the hot guy she was going to have for a student.

CHAPTER 21
NICKNAMES

At this point, you may be wondering about my students. After all, my job was to teach. I did indeed have some fun students. Some of the students I had two years in a row. I wasn't much older than my students, and they were much more engaging than the staff at the Institute.

I don't think the original builders of the Institute, back in 1820, thought about who would be walking the hallowed halls of higher learning, but they definitely could not have imagined Yuri. The Jazz-loving student that carried his guitar to class. He would play in the common area with a gaggle of adoring girls sitting around him. Where Yuri was, Max was not far away. Max was the tall, stoic sidekick. They both loved music and would borrow some of my cassette tapes. Once they asked me to write down the lyrics to *The House of the Rising Sun* by The Animals. Another unwritten task of English teacher volunteers was writing song lyrics for students. *Google* wasn't available, so this task involved listening to cassette tapes over and over on my boom box. I was tempted to write wrong but plausible lyrics, but didn't.

Oksana was a second-year student; therefore, was not a student we taught. However, she was a regular visitor to our dorm rooms. She had been an exchange student in a high school in the States and was up on American slang and speech patterns. She talked fast, and we liked having her around. I remember her being perplexed about why we would willingly leave the States and all it had to offer, for Ukraine. I never did come up with a good explanation.

Roman was often in the company of his three roommates. I would describe Roman as "greasy." His appearance seemed overall greasy (hair, skin, clothes) to me, but he also had a confident demeanor in the way he spoke and his mannerisms. He was relatively handsome, but I was not attracted to him. It was also rumored that he slept his way around the dormitory and had the reputation of a "ladies' man." Given that there were usually four people living in literally one room, I wasn't sure how they worked that out but didn't spend too much time thinking about it. He and his cronies were students in my class during my second year of teaching. I remember Roman mostly because of this one day I was late getting to class. Students were still milling around as I walked my way to the front. Since I was late, I didn't get a chance to take off my pullover raincoat outside the classroom. Unthinking, I pulled the jacket over my head right next to Roman's desk. The expression on his face and the way he exhaled with his hand going to his chest like I was doing a striptease act. It was so repulsive to get a glimpse into his way of hitting on women. I wanted to ask him if that was the way he picked up women and tell him it would never work on American women. But I had a class to teach and just gave him a look of disgust and moved on.

Alla was an outgoing, talkative girl that I would describe as the party girl of the class. She would come by our dorm rooms once in a while. I always felt she was there to gather what information she could about the Americans so she could go back to the student dorm and gossip. Toward the end of the first year, she invited us to a big birthday party she had at the local disco. Jen and I went to the party because we were desperate for a diversion from our every night drudgery. I drank a lot that evening. It was just a few days before Jen was leaving for home and I was already mourning living alone.

Many of my students had the same first name. I could easily have three or four women named Sveta in one class. This necessitated descriptive nicknames so we could differentiate between people and sometimes talk about them when we were in the same room. The students spoke really good English, but if Opal and I spoke quickly, they wouldn't understand.

"Curly Boy" and his roommates, "Village Boy Sasha" and "Chernigov Oleg," soon became regular visitors at our place. During their first visit, a welcome wagon of sorts, the three of them knocked on the door carrying a huge watermelon. We sat around the table eating watermelon and awkwardly trying to make conversation. In an effort to keep the conversation going, I grabbed a little photo album of family and friends I had put together. As they flipped through the pages, I explained what the picture was and who the people were. The last page was a picture I had been given by another student. It was a picture of Jen, my previous roommate, and I at a party the student had at a nearby disco, that we had attended back in the spring. It was a black and white unflattering picture, and I wasn't even looking at the camera, just this mouth closed, surprised look on my face. I made a comment about how bad the picture was, and "Curly Boy" said, "You look beautiful," followed immediately by total silence in the room. No one knew what to say after that kind of statement. I was a little shocked myself. Not only had no one ever said that to me, but he said it with so much conviction that we were all speechless.

The three boys became regular visitors to our kitchen, joined later by Vasiya (no nickname, because he was the only Vasiya we knew). We played Uno and would make burgers, onion rings, even brownies. The guys kept coming back. Whether it was because of our company or the food I made, I don't know. During one evening visit, Curly Boy invited us to his hometown over the upcoming weekend. Before even discussing it, Opal said yes. I was a little hesitant because I knew traveling anywhere in Ukraine was such a pain. In the end, I went along because I thought Curly Boy was cute, and he said that his dad would drive us to his hometown.

On a chilly Friday evening, we crammed into Curly Boy's dad's car. Curly Boy, Vasiya, Opal, Yuri (the dad), and Curly Boy's younger brother. After a couple of hours' drive, we arrived at a small town called Uzeen.

It was a military town with a working Air Force base, one of the largest in Ukraine. There was even a brick wall surrounding the city with sentry posts on several roads leading in and out of the city, leftover from Soviet times, and now standing empty. I couldn't help but think that just a few years ago, I wouldn't have been able to travel to this city, let alone get past the security guard posts. The city wasn't even on maps for security reasons.

Curly Boy's mother had a feast waiting for us with the obligatory shots of vodka. The mother was sweet, and a typical Ukrainian mother worried that we had enough to eat and that we liked her cooking. Scurrying about the kitchen and filling the table with so many plates of food that there wasn't a clear space anywhere on the table. Curly Boy's dad was a retired military man that used to navigate huge bomber airplanes at the nearby military base. I would have never guessed the dad was a military man. He was an energetic person with a hint of mischief and always ready for a shot of vodka. As a gift, I had brought *Planters Cheese Curls* that I was going to give to the family, but before I had given the gift, Curly Boy's dad grabbed them out of my open bag and tried a few with Curly Boy's two younger brothers. I wasn't even mad for the invasion; that's just the kind of person he is. Curly Boy's younger brothers were age fourteen and ten and would only peek around the doorway to watch the Americans. They were too shy to speak in English, Russian, or Ukrainian.

During the day, we wandered around town, checking out the old military planes on display at the military base. Saturday night was "disco" night. We walked down the street to one of the main buildings in the center of town, next to the Lenin statue. Inside was a big gymnasium and a separate room (next to the main entrance) that was the bar. The bar was out of a 1970s dive bar movie: red faux leather booths, wood paneling, and dim lights.

Techno music and some American rock songs blasted the speakers in the darkened gymnasium. The girls dressed in their stiletto heels and short skirts and the guys mostly in tracksuits and/or black leather coats with thick gold or silver chains around their necks. Opal and I stood out in our jeans and sweaters because what girl would wear jeans and sneakers to a disco? The unspoken rule of disco attendance being you can't catch a guy dressing like that. We drank champagne in the bar with some of Curly Boy's friends and then moved to the dance floor. The girls danced wildly in small circles of friends, and for the most part, the guys stood unmoving on the dance floor near their girlfriends, but not dancing. Just standing around, looking tough. Marking their territory, I assume. Curly boy and a few of his friends were the exceptions. They danced along with the girls, having a great time.

Usually, I try to avoid using public restrooms in Ukraine, but with alcohol comes the need to pee. To shamelessly use a quote from the movie *Forrest Gump*, public bathrooms in Ukraine "are like a box of chocolate, you never know what you're going to get." Some of you might be saying to yourself, "Is it that big of a deal?" I have peed in the woods, and on several occasions, a drunken pee in the bushes in-between houses at bar time was not unheard of at my University (hey, it was a long walk from the bars to home- don't judge). Ukraine certainly fits at the low end of the spectrum as far as useable public restrooms. Most of the time, you can't even call them "restrooms" because they more closely resemble pits or holes in the floor in a backroom in an otherwise decent-looking restaurant. I am talking about places where an old-fashioned outhouse would be preferable. That is if you can find a public bathroom to use. No McDonald's to pop into at this time in Ukraine.

If you are walking around the streets of the capital city and need a bathroom, good luck with that. The few bathrooms found required payment to use the facilities. You have to pay a little old lady sitting out front, money for about 4 inches of toilet paper and access to the said bathroom. This puts a damper on the excitement of finding a much-needed public bathroom. The entrance fee was the equivalent of pennies but had to be exact change. No cash back for large or small bills, which can be a problem. The old ladies are strict with their bathroom guarding duties and don't care if you are dancing around about to pee your pants. Americans running past the old ladies, throwing money on the table as they passed, was not an uncommon sight. I never saw a public bathroom in my Ukrainian hometown. I am sure one of the few cafes in town had a bathroom, but I rarely ventured into them.

During training, we had an outing to the ballet theater in the city. We got tickets and in a big group went to the ballet. The theatre was beautiful, old, and ornate. High ceilings, gilded walls, and velvet drapes were a throwback to a different time when high society came to the ballet. We had seats on the balcony, but it was still beautiful. During intermission, several of us went to find the bathrooms. The bathrooms were clean, but to our dismay, it included Turkish toilets with no doors. Turning around quickly, several of us had lost the need to use the facilities. It was almost comical, and we were in shock that such a beautiful and ornate place could have these clean but annoying facilities. Women dressed in long formal dresses and fur coats were in full view, squatting over what was a fancy hole in the floor. That was our introduction to public bathrooms of Ukraine.

The restrooms at the disco, in Curly Boy's hometown, were no different than any other. No stalls and no regular toilets. The only way to know you were in a restroom was because a lot of girls were crammed into a small space, and there was a large mirror on the wall for primping. The "toilets" were on a small platform, up a couple of steps. A crude pedestal with a squat toilet. It was something special, not in a good way, but when you gotta go, you gotta go. At this point, I was tipsy and needed to go; what choice did I have? It takes a special skill set to be able to use the squat toilet and not pee on yourself, made all the more difficult when a couple of cocktails are involved.

Just before Opal and I left the restroom, a petite girl with a platinum blonde bob wig stood in front of us, asking us questions in English. Benign questions that we usually get asked: Why did we come to Ukraine? Did we like living in Ukraine? ..... She seemed to already know that we were guests of Curly Boy. I think the whole town knew that Americans were in town and where they were staying. The girl from the bathroom was excited to practice her English, and we chatted for a few minutes and then continued on our way. Outside the restroom door, Curly Boy was anxiously pacing outside the bathroom door. Nervously coming up to us asking if we were ok and what the girl in the wig had said to us. Confused by his uneasiness, we laughed and said she just wanted to practice her English. Later, we found out that "wig girl" was an ex-girlfriend of Curly Boy.

We continued to dance to the fast songs, and then a slow dance came on. Curly Boy danced with Opal, and I was disappointed. I was hoping he was interested in me. I stood on the edge of the dance floor, trying not to look pathetic. Geez, this was every high school dance in my life flashing before my eyes. Standing on the edge of the dance floor wishing someone would ask me to dance. Then another slow song came on, *Please Forgive Me* by Bryan Adams. Curly Boy had ended his dance with Opal and asked me to dance. We danced slow and close. I pressed my cheek on his and smelled his wonderful, sexy smell. We stayed that way until the song ended. As the dancing came to an end, we walked as a group back to Curly Boy's parent's apartment. Opal and I went to sleep in the living room on a pull-out couch and a fold-out chair. When I went to the bathroom, I passed Curly Boy and Vasiya deep in conversation in the kitchen. They stopped talking when I walked by, as if I could understand what they were talking about. It wasn't hard to figure out, though. Something was going on between me and Curly Boy.

CHAPTER 22
CULTURAL ISSUES

L iving in a fishbowl was an annoying part of life in Ukraine. I spent a lot of time in our suite of dorm rooms, but still, somehow, everyone knew what my roommate and I did, where we went, the clothes we were wearing, and the food we bought. There were some people/volunteers that had a goal of fully blending into the culture that they were living in. They become fluent in the language, knew all the customs, and even tried to dress so they didn't stand out in a crowd. That wasn't going to happen for me. Language fluency wasn't going to happen, and for whatever reason, I stood out in a crowd wherever I went. It wasn't just my clothes that set me apart, although that did play a role. In the land where women walked around all day in heels, I was easy to spot in my athletic shoes or hiking boots. My brown hair was straight and down to the middle of my back. A few Ukrainians came up to me all excited and said, "You are what a real American looks like." I later realized that they thought I was American Indian. As time went on, I started to rebel against the constant watching. Why even try to blend in when everything about me screamed American?

Well into my second year, I didn't even notice the constant watching and attention by people on the street. Sure, if I was feeling especially bold, I would put on a baseball hat when I went to the bazaar for the weekend shopping. People would stare at me, of course. Old ladies would stop in the middle of the street to stare wide-eyed and open-mouthed as I walked by. I am fairly certain my baseball hat-wearing self was a topic of conversation not only at the Institute but in the community in general. Marked on calendars, even. The infamous "Day the American wore a base-ball hat" holiday. Cheers!

In the middle of my second year in Ukraine, my mother had sent me two big boxes of goodies from home. I got a notice that the boxes were waiting at the post office. I asked Curly Boy to go with me to help bring the boxes home. After putting the boxes on a cart I had brought, we started to return to the dorm. We were chatting when we passed a couple of older ladies that were walking the opposite way. After they had passed us, Curly Boy asked, "Does that happen often?"

"Does what happen often?" I replied, oblivious to what had happened.

Apparently, the ladies stopped and stared at me as we passed. I didn't even notice. It was such a regular occurrence. Everything about me stood out. I still think if I wore Ukrainian clothes and somehow hid my hair and didn't say a word, I would still stand out in a crowd.

As part of my teaching load, I created a class on American culture that I taught to the fifth-year students. One of the first things I discussed in the first few classes was stereotypes. I would have my students come up with a list of stereotypes about Americans. The first thing on the list was always-all Americans smile. One look at all the stern, serious people in Soviet photographs, and it was easy to see where they got that idea.

One time I was in Kiev, sitting on a bench in Independence Square, waiting for friends. Two Middle Eastern guys, tourists, were walking around taking pictures. They came up to me, asking questions in a language I didn't recognize. I thought they were asking me to take a picture of them in the square. What they wanted was for me to be in the picture with them. I was hesitant and not sure what was going on but ended up being in their picture. I can just imagine somewhere in Jordan people flipping through their vacation photo album and coming across a picture with me, flashing my confused American smile, awkwardly standing between two strangers. I wonder what these men said about this picture. At least the picture couldn't be used as an example of foreign indecency. I was bundled in my big triple goose down winter coat, jeans, and hiking boots. I have no idea if those two guys thought I was Ukrainian (I doubt it) or some other kind of foreigner.

The second stereotype that students immediately brought up was that all Americans were rich. This was a hard one to dispute, too, with all the American movies on tv, and the few Americans that were in Ukraine had money to buy whatever they needed and wore clothes that the typical Ukrainian could not afford. One day, this led to a very awkward encounter with a student on the street. This male student suddenly appeared as I was walking back from the bank at the main square. Peace Corps deposited a stipend in U.S. dollars in volunteers' accounts every month. The local currency was too unstable to be paid in local money. Every month, I went to the bank to withdraw my stipend. I remembered the student's name, even though his attendance in class was sporadic, because I didn't have a lot of male students. I was also used to random students coming up to me, either my students or one of the first-year students wanting to practice their English with the American. This student went into a story about having no money, and I didn't even realize why he was telling me this until he specifically asked for money from me. When I realized what he was asking for, I said I didn't have any money and quickly walked away. It was unnerving to know that he must have been watching me go into the bank and had waited for me to leave.

I don't have any animosity towards the student that asked me for money or his stereotypical view. From an American cultural point of view, the exchange was awkward and uncomfortable. From a Ukrainian perspective, it was the norm to loan family and friends money, even expected. Considering the crumbling economy in Ukraine at the time, I am surprised that this so-called "rich" American didn't get asked for money more often.

During one trip within Ukraine, the value of Ukrainian money to dollars dropped drastically during a short weekend trip. The currency exchange kiosks could barely keep up with the exchange rates. The signs kept adding zeros to the dollar/Kupon exchange rates. It was during my second year in Ukraine that the Ukrainian government started printing a million kupon bill. It's hard to comprehend, even if you are a witness to the declining buying power of the local currency. The Kupon was the local currency. So, imagine getting one bill for a million Kupons. That is like instead of a $100 bill, having one bill that says $1,000,000.00. It boggled the mind. Try buying a loaf of bread with a price of 20,000 when all you have is a million Kupon bill. It's impossible. No one could give change for that. The bread store, or any store would turn you away. Exact change only!

There were other money-related issues. We (volunteers) were paid in U.S. dollars, which necessitated exchanging those dollars for the local currency. The problem here is that the U.S. dollars had to be in pristine condition. No wrinkles, writing, or blemishes of any kind on the bills. When withdrawing money from the bank, I had to be careful about only taking U.S. dollars in good condition—trying to exchange a less than perfect bill resulted in a rejection of the transaction at the exchange kiosk and being stuck with the unusable bill. On more than one occasion, I shamelessly used my status as an American woman to slip a less than perfect bill through the exchange process. Putting on my biggest American smile, fluffing my long hair and peeking in the tiny exchange kiosk window, I would persistently slide my twenty-dollar bill through the tiny window while saying "I am an American" in Russian, hoping the guy sitting inside would feel sorry for me and exchange my money for the local currency. It worked once or twice. Money could also be exchanged with shady local guys that hung out at the entrance to the bazaar holding big wads of cash. I never attempted a transaction with these guys because I was afraid my math skills wouldn't be fast enough, and I would be on the short end of the deal. Plus, it was illegal to exchange currency on the street.

It was about this time, in my Peace Corps tour, that new and exciting things start showing up in the local bazaar to purchase. I couldn't believe it. First, it was *Butterfinger* and *Baby Ruth* candy bars in certain select kiosks. Then one day, I thought I was having delusions when I found a jar of salsa at the Saturday bazaar. What the heck! *Twinkies* from Turkey, frozen packaged chicken breasts, hot dog packages, and Curly Boy's favorite *Honey Bunches of Oats* cereal. It was amazing to see these things in the open market. There is a good chance that we (Americans) were the only ones to buy these products. The fact that we could have a little taste of home was amazing. Why it took until almost the end of my second year in Ukraine for these things to come on the market, I will never know. I continued my exhaustive search for *Doritos* and peanut butter *M&M's*, but that was a futile effort. Shortages of basic items, like sugar and flour, still made them annoyingly hard to find in the local markets.

CHAPTER 23
UKRAINIAN MEN

From the moment I arrived in Ukraine, I didn't find Ukrainian guys appealing. Granted, during training and to an extent, at the institute I was teaching at, I didn't meet very many Ukrainian men. The ones I saw on the street were almost always smoking and/or spitting on the street from the high tar cigarettes. A group of men drinking vodka and playing cards on a train or at a cafe were to be avoided at all costs. Over the two years, I had been smacked on the butt by a drunk guy walking down the street, harassed by men saying things I couldn't translate but fully understood the meaning, and those overcrowded buses and subways were a pervert's dream come true. There were exceptions, of course. Hearing Russian spoken in a deep, sexy male voice did give me a chill on occasion. Overall, I had resigned myself pretty quickly to the fact that I wasn't going to find my true love in Ukraine.

Halloween came around, and Curly Boy's class at the Institute decided to have a Halloween party and rented out a nearby disco. I racked my brain, trying to come up with a costume that could be made with what we had available. Then I stumbled on an idea as I was browsing through our bookshelves and came across a tourist book on Kiev. One of the main pictures in the book was a statue of the founders of Kiev. Legend has it that around the 15th Century, a family, three brothers and a sister, founded Kiev. This was perfect for Curly Boy, two of his roommates, and myself. Dressed in sheets, toga style, with a blanket thrown over our shoulder and a homemade sign saying the names of each of the founders, we made our way to the Halloween party, careful to distract the dorm monitor lady so she wouldn't see we had used dorm sheets and blankets for our costume. The party was in full swing when we arrived, but we made a big splash with our arrival. The students loved our costumes. It was the talk of the party, and, I am sure, talked about for several days after. If there wasn't any gossip about Curly Boy and his roommates spending so much time with Opal and me, then this party had just upped the ante.

One particular holiday weekend, Opal was the one that needed to get out of town for a little bit. I had just come back from a trip to Poland and was having vivid dreams that I was still on a train rocking back and forth. I stayed back, vowing to tackle the huge pile of laundry that I had accumulated. Before she left, Opal gave me two tickets that a student had given her. They were for some kind of dance show that one of her students was performing in. Not wanting to go to the show by myself, I headed to the student common area in-between classes. I found Curly Boy standing in his green flannel shirt, denim vest, jeans, and cowboy type boots. Tall and handsome as ever. Sigh. I asked if he and his roommates wanted to go to the dance show with me. By this time, a group outing was a typical thing. He said his roommates were planning on going home for the holiday weekend and that he had train tickets home also, but he would get back to me. Later that day, Curly Boy told me that he wasn't going home and would like to go to the dance show. Just like that, it was just him and me going to a dance show. Was this a date? Is this how it worked? I was used to doing group outings, so I wasn't sure what this was.

I wore the one dress I had with a sweater over, and Curly Boy and I walked to the small theater in the center of town. The dance show was a dance recital for ballroom dancing students. Starting with the little kids strutting their stuff in bright costumes, dancing their way across the stage. It took a while for all the students to perform, and the evening ended with the older students, including one or two students from the Institute. We sat in our seats, knees smashed against the seat in front of us because the aisles were so narrow. Shifting every once in a while to get the feeling back in my legs. I was amazed by the talent of these kids. It was late by the time we got out of the concert hall and started walking back to the Institute. Curly Boy offered to make us dinner. I said yes, of course—any excuse to spend more time with this hot guy.

We went back to the house that he was renting with his friends. A big room with three beds pushed up against opposite walls and a small kitchen at the entrance. Curly Boy made a bet that he could go out and buy the ingredients to make a Ukrainian pancake type dish for us. The winner of the bet cooked dinner that night. I took the bet because I knew there was no way he would find all the ingredients on such short notice and being so late in the day. It was hard enough finding things like flour, sugar, eggs, milk during the day. It was at about 8 p.m., and at this point, there was no possible way he was winning this bet. He left to go to the stores on the main square. About 15 minutes later, he came through the door with all the ingredients. Wow! I was shocked until he admitted that he had to ask the neighbor for several of the ingredients. I was right. There was nothing to buy at that time of night. Losing the bet, Curly boy set about making the pancakes, and we sat down to eat with some Champagne. Talking and having a nice time. Toward the end of the night, he asked why I didn't have a boyfriend. Ugh. The dreaded question. Do people think I have an answer to that question?

It was getting late when Curly Boy walked me back to the dormitory. It was a beautiful evening. The moon was shining, and for once, it was not too cold outside. As we walked, I thought, *ok, the two of us have been dancing around the issue but not addressing the attraction between us.* I wasn't even sure if this whole evening was a date. My past unreciprocated crushes made me hesitant to say anything in case Curly Boy didn't feel the same way.

However, that night, walking back, I decided that I needed a kiss goodnight at the door. That's it, step up and just kiss the guy. As we were getting closer to the door, I thought for sure he would turn around and say the usual end of date phrases. A couple of feet from the door, I opened my mouth to say something, but I had no idea what to say. Then before I could stop him, he knocked on the small glass window on the door to the building so that the dormitory hall monitory lady would open the door. She opened the door in two seconds, I swear. My chance for a goodnight kiss was gone, just like that. My mouth still hanging open, I had to walk in the door, and Curly Boy turned around to walk back to his place.

The next morning, Curly Boy showed up at my door, ready to go shopping at the bazaar. The previous night, we had made plans to make an American dinner in my kitchen. Since it was a Saturday, market day, it was easier to get all the ingredients we needed for hamburgers and onion rings. Shopping was so much easier with a native speaker to translate and bargain for whatever was needed. I should have made more of an effort to find a hot guy to translate and shop for me a year ago. Live and learn, as the saying goes. We still had to go to several shops and many stalls at the open market, but we had the makings of a great meal. I also had an enormous mound of laundry to do. It would take me literally all day to hand wash all my clothes in a basin of water that I set in the shower. I didn't think I had that many clothes, and I wore things over and over before finally admitting they needed to be washed.

As I soaked, pounded, wrung out, and cursed my life without a washing machine, Curly Boy asked if he could make cookies. I found the recipe in my handy and only cookbook, showed him where our ingredients were, and he set to work. One of my country music cassette tapes was playing in the background. Mid-wrestling with my laundry, there was a knock on the door. I opened it to one of the dorm monitor ladies that watch over the main lobby of the dormitory. In her hand was a letter for me. I knew who it was from the minute I saw it in her hand. It was from Jake. Yes, green-eyed, handsome, hometown Jake that I had crushed on for longer than I wanted to admit and the same person about whom I told myself over and over again, "Kathy, it's time to move on." He was the only person that copied the Cyrillic return address that I wrote on envelopes sent home, which meant that his letters came to my dorm room. Everyone else wrote the address in English, which was routed to the Institute first, then on to me. I took the letter, closed the door, and quietly went to my room to read what Jake had to say. Curly Boy was in the next room.

Jake's letter was filled with what I interpreted as a slight change of mind towards me. After all, over-analyzing everything was my middle name. He was asking how old I was, like that was hard to figure out since I had been in the same kindergarten class as his youngest brother, who was also his current roommate. He also mentioned that I looked good after my weight loss. Umm, that was a touchy subject for me. What was I, some kind of cyclops before? Then to top it off, he writes that he is happy that his softball team had won the local tournament recently. Duh, I had watched the tournament. Clearly, our make-out session and later when he didn't say goodbye was also missing from his memory of the summer. I put the letter back in the envelope and tossed it aside. Maybe I would answer, but probably not.

The rest of the day passed with Curly Boy and I pleasantly baking and doing laundry. He even volunteered to wring out my washed jeans, one of the most dreaded tasks of handwashing clothes. A definite sign that he was one of the good guys. As it started to get dark outside, we started making dinner—hamburgers, Onion rings, and of course, his cookies for dessert. I also whipped up a batch of my famous *Kool-Aid* and vodka mixers, a sure way to elevate an average evening to a night for the record books. We ate, drank, talked, played cards, and when a good song came on my tape player, we danced in the hallway. Then finally, the moment I had been waiting for, we kissed. Yes! It was everything.

Later, when Curly Boy was leaving, he said maybe the best thing a guy could ever say, "Tomorrow, when you see me, kiss me first, so I know this is real." Sigh.

Chapter 24

Back to the Emerald City

D ating Curly Boy wasn't much different than when we hung out in a group with his roommates and mine. We didn't go on dates; we were just together and inseparable. Most weekends, Curly Boy's roommates would go home, leaving their one-room apartment/house empty. I only stayed there once, though. The only bathroom was an outhouse in the farthest part of the backyard, where there was also a garden. The people that lived on the other side of the house had a bunch of chickens that wandered around the garden at night. If you are thinking: what's the big deal, an outhouse? Then you haven't had to use an outhouse in the middle of the night with no lights in the yard, whatsoever, and live chickens moving around. Being surrounded by live animals that you can't see and also trying to walk across a yard to a place that you don't know where it is or what is in your path is scarier than any haunted house. I'm not even going to mention trying to find the hole in the floor of the outhouse without a light.

The great thing about Curly Boy was that I didn't need to over-analyze everything. We liked each other, that was it. No looking for signs, no trying to interpret gestures or hoping that he liked me. It wasn't all carefree, though. Although no one at the Institute asked me about my relationship with Curly Boy, the gossip was all around me. As a couple, we were a big question mark to the general public. Even his friends, or more specifically, the girlfriends of his friends, were skeptical. Curly Boy had always been a little different as far as clothes, an affinity for travel, and his independence, but dating an American?! That was just incomprehensible. At Curly Boy's birthday party, back in his hometown, I saw the skepticism of me or maybe our relationship.

The birthday party started, as most do, in Curly Boy's parents' apartment with a table loaded with food, bottles of vodka, and surrounded by his closest circle of friends and their girlfriends. While we were eating and making toasts, I looked at the other end of the table, and two of the girlfriends were whispering to each other and looking at me with looks of ... hmm, how to describe the looks they were giving me? I guess, to me, their whispering and looks conveyed a feeling of "you are taking one of our men, and what's so great about you?" This didn't surprise me. I had noticed over the last year and a half a surprising lack of "sisterhood" between Ukrainian women. By that, I mean that many women saw each other as competition rather than a friend or support. I think this happens everywhere in the world, and I had an understanding of why there was a lack of sisterhood. The women were in a male-dominated society and felt they had to compete with other women to get the man that would take care of them or make their lives better. I am not an expert in the socio-economical psychology of women in society, just an observer of what was happening at that time and place.

On the other end of the spectrum, dating Curly Boy caused discomfort with Opal, my roommate, too. I had a boyfriend, and she didn't. I didn't want to do the typical girl thing and drop my friends, but I also wanted to spend time with my new man. I didn't want things to be weird with Opal because I understood where she was coming from. I had been the third wheel when my friends had boyfriends, and I didn't want her to feel that way. However, the sight of her shocked expression when I told her I wasn't coming back to the dorm one night, followed by her knocking on Curly Boy's door early the next morning, was awkward. It wasn't until months later, when I had borrowed her suitcase, that I found a half-written letter that she had written to her sister that questioned my relationship and compatibility with Curly Boy because he was younger than me. I am sure she had just written down what a lot of people were thinking, and I didn't dwell on it.

Yes, you read that correctly. Curly Boy was younger than me. Five years younger, to be exact. On paper, we were not a match. Age difference, culture difference, country of origin difference, and even family background was different. Curly Boy's parents were still married, and he had two younger brothers. I, on the other hand, have a wonderfully blended family that required a map to explain our relationship to each other. He had a series of long term, monogamous relationships from a young age. And, well, if you have been reading up to this point, you already know about my romantic stumbles and misses. Plenty of fodder for gossip and reasons why we wouldn't be a good match. All of that really didn't matter. I loved that Curly Boy would do little things for me, like buying me a *Twinkie* (made in Turkey) for no reason at all. The cultural differences were an advantage too. The male-centered society brought out a chivalrous behavior towards women, at least it did for Curly Boy. I was always relieved of carrying anything heavy, was protected from unwanted attention, and treated like I was delicate, which, given my well-rounded size, was something I had never felt before, and I liked it. And he was handsome as all get out, whew, superficial but true. Being an American and all the differences that implies was initially an attraction for Curly Boy. Everything about me was different and made me stand out in a crowd, and he obviously liked that. The more time we spent together, the more similarities we found, too. We both found the same things funny, had a similar outlook on most subjects, and had the same thoughts on future family and ideals. I can only guess what was said when we were out of hearing range, but sometimes you have to say fuck that and do what you want.

Thanksgiving was done up right that year, too. Opal and I invited Curly Boy and his roommates, plus a few of our favorite students, to a feast on Thanksgiving day. However we still had classes to teach that day. An American holiday wasn't a day off in Ukraine, weird. My culinary skills were put to the test this day. A feast was made with things as close to the typical Thanksgiving fair as we could get. Chicken instead of Turkey, potatoes, salads, the works. All made on our one hot plate and our easy bake oven. The Ukrainians tried everything, and we all had a good time. Of course, the guys were forced to do the dishes.

Early on, Opal and I set the rule that whoever cooks doesn't do the dishes. Which meant that the guys had to do the dishes. Take that ingrained in Ukrainian society gender-defined roles; we don't do that here. Get to scrubbing, boys.

With the success of our Thanksgiving, we decided to undertake Christmas, but this time, invited volunteers from our training group. Four of them decided to make the trek to Nizhyn for the holiday. Preparations were exhausting. Endless shopping and menu preparations. We even arranged for a hotel stay for some of the group because we only had room for one extra person in our dorm rooms. Everyone arrived and had a good time. Curly Boy and his roommates cut down a tree in the park, under the cover of darkness, that we put in our hallway. I set up my empty cheese curl cans in a pyramid with homemade paper decorations on them. I knew I would find a use for them. In advance, we told people we were having a tacky gift exchange. Everyone brought the tackiest thing they could find, which wasn't too hard to find in Ukraine. The winner had brought an empty *Miller Lite* can. How he found that in Ukraine is really surprising, but he did live in Kiev, after all. A much larger selection of goods than in my adopted hamlet.

This year was my second holiday season in Ukraine, and it was quickly decided we needed to be in Poland, specifically Kracow. The land of colors, restaurants, and everything we held near and dear to our hearts- pork flavored potato chips for everyone. Yeah! Dorothy may have said, "there is no place like home," but this Emerald City had almost everything we needed to refresh, restore, and reinvigorate our souls. Kathleen, Sherri, and Jen had left the Peace Corps by this time, which left Opal, Marie, and myself.

It wasn't a want; it was a necessity to take a break from Ukraine and renew our energy in Kracow, Poland.

I can almost see the thoughts and questions spinning in your head: After all the travel disasters that have happened to this chick, why would she possibly want to put herself through that yet again? The answer was desperation mixed with just plain craziness. This was my second year living in Ukraine, and coping strategies had been developed. One of the main coping mechanisms, besides drinking, was getting the hell out of Ukraine, no matter what. Even if it was just for a few days, it wasn't a want but a desire. It could even be considered a necessity. This trip, I asked Curly Boy if he wanted to join us, promising him McDonald's and all the wonders of Poland.

Right after Christmas, we boarded the train and relaxed for our trip to Poland. The conductor came through as usual to check our tickets and sell the sheet sets for our bunks. The sheet set cost less than a dollar, worth the price for nice clean sheet sets sealed in a clear plastic bag. We received one sealed sheet set that included a pink washcloth and three opened sheet sets without the pink washcloth. The conductor handed out the sheet packets, giving the sealed one with the pink washcloth to Curly Boy. We noticed the pink washcloth discrepancy and joked about the Ukrainian getting the only pink washcloth, but soon forgot about it. Our vacation had started. Relaxing, reading, and sleeping were all we wanted on this long train ride. It was a direct route- Kiev to Kracow. No switching trains and just a simple Polish border crossing. At least, that is what it was supposed to be.

It was early morning when we arrived at the Ukrainian border. The sun was just coming up. There was the usual commotion of the border guards as they rushed about checking the train for contraband and checking the passports of the passengers. They arrived at our cabin and quickly checked, stamped and gave back passports for Opal, Marie, and myself. Curly Boy's passport, they took down the hall to discuss with the other guards. The guard came back a few minutes later and called Curly Boy out into the corridor. After some discussion, Curly Boy relayed to me that he was told he had to get off the train. Although he had a Ukrainian passport for international travel, he did not have a special stamp in his passport allowing him to leave the country. I was stunned and scared for him. I asked if I could get off the train with him. Curly Boy said the guards wouldn't let me get off. We had a hurried goodbye, and slowly, he turned around, grabbed his backpack, and followed the guard off the train. I stood there helpless, not sure what to do and not sure what was going to happen to Curly Boy. I still hoped that he would get this "special stamp" in his passport and meet us later in Krakow. Not sure why I chose this time to think that anything in Ukraine would be easy and quick.

Sad and worried about Curly Boy, the train continued. We passed the Polish border and continued to Krakow. Opal, Marie and I were more than ready to get off the train when we arrived in Krakow later that afternoon. We gathered our things together and returned the sheet sets to the conductor. With the hustle and bustle of all the passengers getting ready to get off the train, we didn't pay much attention to the conductor asking about three missing pink washcloths. We blew it off as just another weird train thing. We lined up with the other passengers in the hallway to get off the train at the Krakow station. The conductor became more and more vocal, yelling in Russian about the missing towels. A conductor from another train car soon joined in on the ruckus that had started, blocking our way off the train until we paid $20 for the missing towels.

Marie, Opal, and I lost it at this point. Both sides yelling and screaming. We refused to pay for the so-called "missing towels," and the conductors insisting we pay. We even tried yelling out the train car window to try to get the attention of the police or anyone that could help. The conductors would not budge. Then the train started moving, and this jolted us into panic mode. The train was going on to Warsaw, and we couldn't get off. The conductor ran over to pull the emergency brake, and the entire train came to a halt, still at the station. They finally gave up and let us off the train, and on the platform was a police officer. We went up to him and pleaded our cases. The three of us gesturing and trying to explain what happened. The Police officer stood stoically pacifying us with benign questions as another police officer boarded the train and exited a few minutes later with a couple of bottles of vodka under his coat. As soon as the vodka toting police officer passed us, there was nothing left to do. We moved on down the train platform and out of the train station.

I had hoped that Curly Boy would make it to Poland, but he never did. Once he was taken off the train, I had no idea where he went or what had happened to him. Was he being held in a cell somewhere at the border, or did he make his way home? It put a damper on the fun of Kracow. We even went to a U.S. consulate office in Kracow to report our train/washcloth extortion scheme. We talked to the main guy at the consulate, but there was nothing much that could be done. He said we were lucky to still have our passports, telling us a story of another Peace Corps volunteer that was strategically pushed around as he was getting on a train in order to get his passport. The victim in the story happened to be from our group. The whole experience made us jaded. Here we were in Ukraine trying to help and do something good, and we had turned into targets. It was also a reminder of what a lot of us felt, that life in Ukraine had gotten more dangerous. The economy and desperation of some people made Americans a lucrative target. For whatever reason, probably because the Ukrainian currency had become more and more unstable, we, as American volunteers, felt more unsafe during our second year than our first. We only spent a few days in Poland, and I was ready to go back to Ukraine.

Before I boarded the train home, I stopped at McDonald's to buy a few cheeseburgers for the road. It was a quiet 18-hour trip back to Kiev. I didn't know when or if I would see Curly Boy. We had no way to communicate. No cell phones, and no email. The school was on winter break. The guards had escorted him off the train so quickly that we didn't have time to discuss when or where we were going to meet up. The snow was falling in the early evening when the train pulled into the Kiev train station. It was an uneventful trip back, but I was still tired. As I stepped off the train, there on the platform was Curly Boy holding a single red rose. How he knew what train I would be on and what time it was coming in, I still don't know till this day. I was so happy to see him. We shared a long kiss on the platform. Curly Boy ate those McDonald's cheeseburgers with such happiness and enthusiasm, despite sitting in the paper bag for well over 24 hours.

CHAPTER 25
"I DO"

Things with Curly Boy moved fast. We spent all our free time together. The incident with the trip to Poland only made us want to be together more. In January, he found an apartment to rent, and we moved in together. A nice two-room place, not far from the Institute, that had no furniture. Only a kitchen sink, stove, and refrigerator. We had to sneak the mattresses out of my dorm room, past the dorm monitor ladies, so we could have something to sleep on. I put a blanket on the floor in the bedroom as my dresser. A kitchen counter was made with a scrap piece of wood and a crate. Later on, the landlord must have felt sorry for us and brought in a couch and table for the second room. We didn't have much, but we were happy.

Our lives took on a new routine. I was still teaching my classes, and Curly Boy was going to his classes. No one said anything to us about our new living arrangements, not that I thought they would. Curly Boy's English was always good, but speaking English all the time made it better. Although, he did run into trouble with his teachers at the Institute, for speaking American English rather than the required British English. For example, he got in the habit of using the American pronunciation of the word "can't" instead of the British variation: the result, a lower grade and probably an increase in gossip among the teachers.

Meanwhile, my Ukrainian got worse and worse. I didn't need to work on my language skills when I had a sexy translator with me all the time. My innate laziness was also a contributing factor. I think Curly Boy inherited his haggling skills from his mother. Over time, we probably saved a lot of money. No more paying the American or foreigner prices in the bazaar or at small tables of goods set up on the street. Curly Boy negotiated with all the sellers at the local market and didn't just accept the first price offered, as I did. A common practice for some sellers is to give a higher price when they realize the buyer is a foreigner. Not all vendors price-gouged. Our regular pickle selling lady would make fun of Curly Boy's hair and sell her delicious pickles for the same price as usual.

It was great having our own apartment. We spent time cooking and having the occasional party with our regular group of friends/students. We were definitely not living in the lap of luxury because we still had to hand wash our clothes in the bathtub. At least we had a bathtub, which was a step up from the shower in the dorm. Besides having a random old lady from the building trying to push her way into the apartment, it was a quiet place to live. I am guessing the old lady thought it was her apartment, but not sure why she thought she had to push her way past strangers, and a stranger speaking weird Ukrainian, to get into her apartment.

When I was living in the dormitory, there were regular rotating shifts of stoic Ukrainian ladies monitoring the main door of the building and vigilantly watching over who could go down the hall to knock on our door. I took these ever-present ladies for granted and moved out of the dorm rooms with a naive view of my own security. This particular day was like every other day. Curly Boy had left the apartment for his classes before me. We were expecting a guest later that night, so I tidied up and unknowingly put pillows over my only big-ticket item, my camera. Out the door, I went for my classes an hour after Curly Boy, locking both locks on the door behind me.

Curly Boy arrived home before I did, to a door that had only ONE lock locked and an apartment that had been torn apart. Not sure why the apartment was way more disheveled than when he left that morning, it took him a few minutes to realize that we had been robbed. Taking the big shopping bag I kept near the front door, the burglar had cleaned us out. Not much left but a dusty outline on the table where my boombox used to be and an empty ring box from a sentimental ring that Curly Boy had given me for Christmas. In shock, he called the police, and I arrived home to an apartment full of police officers milling around the rooms. My first call was to the Peace Corps office to report the crime. Their only response was to ask if my passport had been taken. My pleas of feeling unsafe because the police had completely taken off one of the locks on the door and left a hole in the door were met with "Oh, you can just call someone to fix the door." Yeah, maybe in the capital city a door can be fixed within the hour on a late Friday afternoon, but not in my small berg.

To make it even more ridiculous, a few days later, all my students in the class I was teaching during the robbery (all female) were asked down to the police station and fingerprinted. To recap, the thief watched Curly Boy leave our apartment, watched me leave our apartment, and probably knew when we were scheduled to return. Then Nizhyn's finest decided the most likely suspects in this well-planned caper were a group of 19-year-old women that were seated directly in front of me during the break-in. Hey, at least I still had my camera hidden under the pillows, and my clothes were decidedly not the robber's style.

On most weekends, we would also go to Curly Boy's parents' apartment for various gatherings and planned parties. Those trips were almost always the same. Curly Boy's mom would make a ton of wonderful food. She knew what dishes I liked best and would have everything ready when we arrived. His mom didn't speak English but instead communicated through enormous amounts of food. After eating, we would head to the home of the only friend that had his own apartment. Really it was the friend's parents' apartment, but the parents were never home. This was the main reason we started and ended the night at this place. In between, we would go to the local disco to dance and drink.

Curly Boy's friends wouldn't speak English to me until they had reached a certain level of intoxication. At that point, they were fluent, giving a toast and asking me questions in English. Alcohol tends to be a great fear eliminator—no worrying about grammar rules and correct pronunciation. Just say anything you know. This led to one of Curly Boy's friends saying a memorable phrase one late night, "(Curly Boy), he is hungry like a wolf." English wasn't this guy's expertise, but thanks to alcohol and the European rock group, *Duran, Duran*, he said what he knew and also bonded us together with a fun catchphrase.

Not sure if it was an unofficial rule or what, but it seemed like the majority of volunteers that stuck it out over the two years had found a mate, usually a Ukrainian. Every time I ran into a fellow volunteer, I heard about someone getting married. Long before *90 Day Fiancé* was a hit tv show, Curly Boy and I had our version. Having heard about the lengthy visa process from other volunteers, I brought up the topic of marriage. Curly Boy's response was he needed to go home the upcoming weekend and talk to his parents. When he came back, he said he talked to his parents, and he wanted to get married. When we told his mom, she cried but was happy. Plans were underway for our wedding in Ukraine. Curly Boy's dad sold his car to pay for the wedding celebrations, and his mom was busy making arrangements for a traditional Ukrainian three-day plus wedding.

Now, it was time to tell my family. I had written to them that I had a boyfriend, but they didn't know how serious it was. On Valentine's Day, I sent a fax saying that I would be calling the following weekend to my parent's house. Yes, you read that correctly. I sent a fax. The Institute had a fax machine. A prized possession of the English Department, although I don't think it was used very often. Early in my first year, I had wanted to use the fax machine to make some plans with a few of the other volunteers. No amount of talking would persuade Oleksander that faxes could be handwritten. He instead told me to go to the office of the secretary of the English Department to type my fax before it could be sent. As soon as I walked into the office, the sweet, young assistant asked me if I wanted to use the "printer." What? Stop everything. I became giddy with the thought of using a computer and printing out my letter to be faxed. I didn't see any computers in the room, but I practically danced in the doorway anyway. My hopes fell quickly as the secretary showed me to the desk with a typewriter sitting on top. Defeated, I accepted my fate and started typing. Ugh. It took forever. I almost failed typing class in high school, so I knew this wasn't going to go well. I knew the supply of correction tape was limited, so I tried to be careful with using it. Little rectangular pieces of film that are coated in *White Out* that is used to correct mistakes by retyping over the characters, for those that have no idea how typewriters work.

It took me most of the afternoon to get a page "printed" out. When I gave it to Oleksander, I again had to use all my skills of persuasion to tell him that a fax with mistakes crossed out on it was ok to send. Either he didn't send the fax, or it never made its way through the Ukrainian telephone lines. However, the fax to my family mysteriously made it to its destination, maybe because that fax was shorter with fewer mistakes.

It was expensive to call home, and I had only done it a few times. It also involved going to Oleksander's apartment so that he could make arrangements with the local telephone office to put the call through. Most of the time, we had to wait for a half-hour or more for the telephone company to call back before finally being connected to the person we were calling. Did you really think I could call America directly? I was nervous about calling my family. Curly Boy was my first boyfriend, and I generally kept my romantic interests to myself. To take the pressure off me explaining to my parents that I was getting married, I convinced Curly Boy that it was an American tradition to ask the parents for the daughter's hand in marriage. Technically, it is a tradition, so I didn't really stretch the truth that far. That's my story, and I am sticking to it. I'm counting on you all to keep my minor exaggeration to yourselves. Wink, Wink. Nudge, Nudge.

At the appointed time, Curly Boy and I walked to Oleksander's apartment and started the phone call. Before I knew it, I was talking to my dad, step-mother, and little sister all on three separate landline extensions and then handed the phone to Curly Boy. My family giggled, and my dad welcomed Curly Boy to the family. If they had reservations about my international love connection, they kept it to themselves. The next call was to my mother, who had a more reserved response. Can't blame her; it was not the courtship and marriage that she envisioned for her only daughter.

Arrangements were in progress, the family had been called, and besides sending out invitations, my only responsibility was getting a wedding dress. I didn't think I would find anything I liked or that would fit in the very few bridal stores available in Ukraine. I scoured magazines, mostly *People* magazines, for wedding gown designs that I could show to the person that was going to make my wedding gown. The seamstress was amazing and could make any dress I wanted from a picture. I did have to provide the material, thread, and any other dress trimming that would be needed. Curly Boy and I took a day and headed to Kiev for wedding dress material shopping.

The stereotypes of customer service in the former Soviet Union, or should I say lack of customer service, is not only true but alive and still going on today. Going into a store and not remembering it was break time was always confusing. It was not unusual to find an older saleswoman sitting on a chair next to the counter staring blankly out into space as you approach to ask for a product in the store. Without moving a muscle or changing her stare, the store clerk just says "pererva" (break time) as you sheepishly walk back out of the store.

The quintessential example of shopping in post-Communist times happened while buying lace trim for my wedding dress. If this had happened when I was shopping on my own, I would have chalked it up to one of those things that happened to Americans, but I was with my then Ukrainian fiancé. The whole "American" theory was out the window. The story begins at the biggest and most well-known department store in Kiev, located in the middle of the city on the main street, Khreschatyk Street. I needed some lace for around the neckline of my wedding dress. We were at the counter perusing the lace, and after looking at a few bolts that were on shelves behind the counter, I decided on the one I wanted, and Curly Boy told the salesclerk that we wanted the equivalent of one yard of lace, to which the expressionless clerk told us we first had to pay the cashier at the other end of the counter as she returns the bolt of lace to the shelf. Since the entire counter area was empty of customers, we had no trouble walking the eight steps to the cashier. Of course, we had to wait while the cashier finished her conversation with her co-worker and grudgingly came over to take our money. Receipt in hand, we walked the eight steps back to the same salesclerk standing where we had left her less than a minute ago. We handed the receipt to the same salesclerk. Instead of having the lace cut and ready to go, we got a blank stare and a "What do you want?" from the surly salesclerk. We looked at her in amazement as our jaws dropped to the ground.

"What do you mean, what do we want?" my now-husband sarcastically asked the clerk. "What do you think we want?"

Shaking our heads and laughing at the absurdity of the situation, we asked again for the lace and walked away.

A little over a month after we were engaged, we were escorting a bunch of my fellow volunteers to the bus station in Kiev, on our way to Curly Boy's hometown for the wedding festivities. We were able to reserve rooms in a military hotel for most of the out-of-town guests. My room-mate, Opal, fellow volunteer, Marie, a Ukrainian teacher/friend, Olga, and myself were staying the night before the wedding in an apartment across the hall from Curly Boy's parents' apartment. There were two bedrooms in the apartment. One had a large king-size bed, and the other room had a small twin bed. All our things were in the large bedroom as we got ready to go to sleep that night.

I took a quick bath, and when I returned, I noticed Marie wasn't in the room but didn't think much of it until Opal said that while I was in the bathroom, Marie was whining and complaining. Opal told her to go ahead and take the other bedroom for the night. I couldn't even believe that a.) Opal would tell Marie to take the room and b.) Marie would think it was ok to have a room all to herself the night before MY wedding. I was shocked. I thought about storming in the room and asking what the hell she was thinking. In the end, I wasn't the bridezilla type, and I didn't want to create drama or conflict. So, the night before MY wedding, I shared a bed with two other people. I say shared a bed because who can sleep the night before their wedding, especially with two other people in the same bed? I mean, really, who does that?

I was still resentful of the sleeping situation the next morning, but too much was going on to dwell on it. The morning was a blur of doing my hair, getting dressed, and waiting. A traditional Ukrainian wedding starts with the groom bargaining for the bride. Since my parents were not there, negotiations were held with my maid of honor, Opal. As a small group of the wedding guests watched, my soon-to-be husband recited a poem, offered a trinket he knew Opal liked, and paid the equivalent of 50 cents in Ukrainian money. That's it. That was my bride price. I'm not sure if I should have been happy or sad about my husband's bargaining skills. The deal was sealed, and the dowry paid, now we could get married. We left the apartment building with people sprinkling us with water and throwing coins, all for good luck. Outside the building, a table with a bucket of water was set up. It was the start of many traditional wedding rituals that happened over the three days of festivities. Many words were said, wishes were made for a good marriage- that is what I am guessing anyway- Curly Boy didn't translate most of what was said. Water was a symbol of good luck, so we were supposed to sip (or pretend to sip) from the bucket of water. I pretended to sip the water but did put my lips to the ladle. That mistake will come into play on day two of the wedding ceremony.

We headed, in cars decorated with baby dolls strapped to the hood (another tradition I didn't understand), to the building where the equivalent of a civil ceremony would be held. Technically, we were married the day before in the capital city of the region. The people in the local government office in Curly Boy's small town weren't sure what to do with an American/Ukrainian wedding. They said they couldn't do the official paperwork. We had to go to the regional capital city and do an abbreviated version of the ceremony the day before. Our witnesses that day happened to be Curly Boy's dad and his best friend, Alex, for the pre-ceremony ceremony. This was the first of what was to be many bureaucratic hoops that we had to jump through as a newlywed couple.

On this day, we were going through a ceremony for our friends and family. The civil ceremony was all about theatrical staging and traditions, officiated by a woman with hair piled high on her head, bouffant style, and a long, formal dress. She was the Ukrainian Vanna White of the wedding circuit. The ceremony was relatively uneventful. I had no idea what "Vanna" was saying. At one point, Curly Boy and I were supposed to step on a specially made embroidered cloth, similar to a table runner that was put on the floor. I had been warned about this beforehand because there was a superstition that whoever stepped on the towel first would be the boss of the house. I knew that part of the ceremony was coming up but didn't know when was the official time to step. Curly Boy beat me to the towel by two seconds. The crowd of wedding guests let out a small giggle.

After Curly Boy nudged me when I needed to say I do, we were officially husband and wife. We headed to the wedding reception after some photo ops and dropping off flowers at a local war monument—another traditional part of the wedding festivities. There were about fifty guests at the wedding. Most of whom I didn't know, but about ten of my fellow Peace Corps volunteers came to celebrate with us. Everyone sat at one long horseshoe-shaped table. The table was heavy with food, bottles of homemade vodka, and bottles of champagne at regular spacing on the table.

The night was a loop of eating, a guest making toasts to the bride and groom, drinking (of course), dancing, then starting the routine all over again until all the guests had made a toast. It was a long night. My friends/fellow Peace Corps volunteers were my surrogate family that day. I knew it was going to be hard to get married without my family there, but my fill-in family made it a little less sad. Since my family wasn't there, I had asked the husband of one of the married couples from my Peace Corps group to be my surrogate Dad that day. He made a nice toast and even got choked up a little. Of course, the copious amounts of alcohol helped everyone let loose and have fun. The reception started with all the American volunteers sitting on one end of the table and the Ukrainians sitting at the other. At the end of the night, everyone was mingling and vowing to be best friends for life. Language barrier? Not a problem with the right amount of alcohol.

The merriment started again on the second day. Everyone returned to the reception hall and did a shot of homemade vodka just so they could gain entrance to the venue; it was a little sneak peek of how day two of the wedding was going to go. More eating, drinking, and general merriment ensued. Unfortunately, I got so sick I had to leave day two of the wedding party early. Thank goodness Curly Boy's parents lived in a nearby apartment with a fully functioning bathroom. My suspicion was the water we had to pretend to drink before the wedding ceremony, but it could have been anything. It was Ukraine, after all. Before too long, it was time for the American volunteers to catch the bus back to Kiev. Saying goodbye to their new best friends, the volunteers got into two vans headed to the bus station, but not before the Ukrainians ran outside with a tray of vodka shots for the road. It would be rude to refuse- what's a dedicated volunteer to do?

The third day of the wedding festivities is for the parents, so Curly Boy and I went back to Nizhyn, and things went back to normal. Although I had never made any kind of official announcement that I was getting married, it was general knowledge around the Institute. I am sure the rumors of Curly Boy and I dating and getting married started long before we got together. Just a few days after the first date/dance recital, Curly Boy and I decided to go for a walk. It was the first snowfall of the season. We had just left the dormitory and walked side by side along a path around the building. The first and only person we walked past that day was the biggest gossip of the English Language students. I knew then that the rumors would spread fast.

Knowing that if Curly Boy and I wanted to go to the U.S. together that summer, extensive amounts of paperwork needed to be completed. A complicated process of filling out forms and getting stamps and signatures from both the U.S. Embassy and Ukrainian government offices. We took a whole day in Kiev to get the paperwork done but still needed a second day to finish. First, we started at the U.S. Embassy. My U.S. passport allowed us to get into the Embassy to get the necessary paperwork and stamps from the embassy people behind the bulletproof glass windows.

On our first trip to the Embassy, Curly Boy and I almost inadvertently created an international incident. We arrived at the Embassy, and before getting to the glass service window, all people have to go through the security office. Curly Boy had a backpack with him, and the security guard asked to look through it. We handed it over without a second thought and didn't even really think about what, if anything, was in the backpack. The guard pulls out a can of shaving cream (bought early that morning), a roll of duct tape (still don't know why we had that), and my Swiss army knife. We laughed, realizing that these items must look like we were planning a spy movie type assault on the Embassy. The guard smiles and says he will keep those items there in the security office while we were inside. We quickly agreed. International incident averted. Whew!

Taking the U.S. Embassy papers, we headed to a Ukrainian government office for the next step in the process. Waiting in line for a little bit, we handed over the papers to a dour woman behind the counter. She quickly looked over the papers and immediately handed them back to me, saying they were no good. At this point, we had spent more than half the day waiting in various lines and going all over Kiev, getting paperwork and stamps. I start arguing, sliding the paperwork back across the counter, demanding to talk to a supervisor. Both sides of the counter getting angry. The woman said the stamp on our paperwork wasn't valid because the U.S. Embassy had put two stamps on the paperwork. One stamp was a partial stamp, and then they added a second full stamp. Both were the same stamp. Obviously to all, that only part of the stamp had shown the first time, necessitating a second full stamp. No amount of arguing was going to persuade this remnant of soviet stoic bureaucracy that the stamp was legal. We had no choice but to trudge all the way to the U.S. Embassy and start all over. New stamp (just one this time) on a new form. This time, it passed the test, and on to the next stamp on the form.

The next office we had to go to must have employed the twin sister of the first office. Curly Boy went into the office and was turned away because it was the end of the day. Working close to closing time- yeah, not going to happen. He went the next weekend to try his luck again. This time, he brought with him a bottle of champagne and a chocolate bar. Bingo. The women welcomed him with open arms, and our paperwork was complete. Or at least the pre-paperwork that was needed to start the U.S. visa process.

CHAPTER 26

HONEYMOON

My last semester teaching came to an end, and Curly Boy and I were waiting for his U.S. visa. Plenty of time to take a honeymoon. We found cheap bus tickets to Turkey. Unknown to me at the time, this was the first clue to my husband's lifelong love of traveling as frugally as possible. A 36-hour bus trip started with enthusiasm but soon evolved into a tedious nightmare. The bus didn't have a bathroom. Instead, the bus would make random stops in places along the route- sometimes restaurants and sometimes just pulling over on the side of the road. This bus and many, many other tourist buses all pulled over next to the same roadside bushes. Gross, to say the least. There is a reason this particular tour company is not mentioned in any travel guides. I did see some nice sights while traveling down the highway, such as the horses with bright ribbons on their bridle and wagon trotting down the road in Romania.

It was the middle of the night when the bus drove up to the Bulgarian border. A few days before we got on the bus, we followed the advice in my *Let's Go Europe* and went to the Bulgarian Embassy in Kiev for a visa in my American passport. At the Embassy, I paid the fee, and they put a visa stamp in my passport and gave it back with a scrap of paper. Curly Boy asked what the little piece of paper was for and was told it was nothing, just a receipt.

Back to the Bulgarian border. I was the only American on a bus full of Ukrainians, all women going to buy products in Turkey for resale in

Ukraine; this made me stand out more than usual. Sure enough, I was called off the bus for a visa issue with my passport. Curly boy wasn't allowed to go with me as he didn't need a visa. The armed guards were silent as they escorted me to the border patrol building. I wonder if they knew the Belorussian border guard? Were my past failed border crossings considered a local issue, or did I now have an Interpol file? Hmmm. Arguing with the borders guards was useless once again. You would think I would have learned my lesson the first time this happened or at least the second time. The guards told me that I didn't have a receipt for my Bulgarian visa, rendering what I did have useless. Yep, that's right. That little scrap of "useless" paper cost me another $30 at the border. What am I, a magnet for armed border guards and visa issues? After pacing in front of the counter in the border office and paying the fee, I was escorted back to the bus and the unfortunate sight of one of the three bus drivers beaten to a pulp by the border guards. Not sure the reason why the bus driver was beaten up, but they said it was a regular occurrence and the reason why they had three drivers for the bus. Rumor on the bus was the Bulgarians hated Turkish bus drivers. We continued with the bus trip, and it solidified our decision to buy plane tickets for the return trip to Ukraine.

Turkey was exotic with the bonus of being affordable on our limited budget. After easily finding a cheap hotel, we spent the next couple of days wandering the Grand Bazaar and visiting the local tourist attractions, mostly the famous mosques. While wandering around the outside of the Blue Mosque, a man approached us, telling us that it was prayer time and not to go inside the Mosque. We hadn't planned on going inside the Mosque, but thanked him for the information and started to walk away. The man said, "Wait, come with me," insisting that we follow him around the side of the building. Naive to the workings of the local salespeople, we followed as he kept waving us forward. It wasn't until we were inside his small store that we realized it was all a sales technique for tourists to buy a handmade Turkish rug. We had admired the handwoven rugs that we had been seeing in Istanbul, so we played along.

Sitting down and accepting the offered traditional sweet apple tea, the carpets were laid in front of us. Piled higher and higher until we saw a few we liked. When our choice was narrowed down, the negotiations began. It was comical to hear the salesman say what a good price the rug was and that his prices were the best because his store didn't have a lot of overhead, while my husband responded by pleading poverty because he was a student and couldn't possibly afford very much. This back and forth continued for a long time until finally, an agreement was made, and we carried the rolled-up rug out of the store.

Despite our misgivings about riding another bus, we did end up riding the bus along the coast of Turkey to a resort town called Kusadasi. The bus was clean, big, and included a bathroom on board. Whew. However, the Turkish way of dealing with smokers was to have designated areas for them, including on buses and airplanes, as we would later find out. And by designated area, I mean an area, a couple of rows of seats, in the front of the bus where the smokers could sit and smoke the entire trip. No barrier, no walls, no partitions, just the seats in front where people could smoke as the smell and resulting smoke rolled through the entire bus. What exactly was the purpose of a smoking section anyway?

Arriving in Kusadasi was the Turkish equivalent of Daytona Beach. Small hotels, bars, souvenir shops, and restaurants everywhere, mostly catering to European vacationers. Signs outside restaurants advertised a real "English Breakfast," and the bars offered nightly drink specials. We spent most of our time on the beach. It was crowded but allowed the opportunity to meet people from all over the world, like the older couple from Scotland that was sitting next to me. The male was very talkative, but I couldn't understand a word he was saying. At one point, I looked over at my husband and asked him what the heck this Scottish guy was saying. He didn't have a clue either, but English was his second language. I guess he had an excuse. I did a lot of nodding and smiling.

As all good things come to an end, so must our excursion. We returned to Ukraine tanned and relaxed with our Turkish rug and various other trinkets from our travels. Now, all we had to do was wait for the U.S. visa to come through. My husband stayed with his parents while I helped out at the Peace Corps office during the week and headed to my in-laws' on the weekend.

WRAPPING IT ALL UP, SORT OF

After what seemed like an eternity, we finally had an appointment to go to the U.S. Consulate to get a visa. We were finally going home, or more correctly, I was going home with my new husband. I was excited to be going home and starting a new life again, this time with a partner. Together.

First, my husband and I headed to Warsaw for our visa appointment at the U.S. consulate. After some teary goodbyes with friends and family, we boarded a train for Krakow, then another to Warsaw. As we crossed the Ukraine/Polish border, we both let out a huge sigh of relief and uncrossed our fingers. It was smooth and easy, just how it was supposed to be.

After running around Warsaw with visa paperwork, we finally arrived at the Embassy for our appointment. Everyone waited in one large room for their name to be called up to the row of glass window partitions, separating the non-U.S. people from the Embassy people. It was a big group of people all hoping for their U.S. visas.

One particular couple stood out. A young girl in her early twenties being ordered around by a loudmouth, arrogant guy with a cowboy hat and cowboy boots wearing a cheap polyester suit. Ordering the girl to walk here or there and sit in that chair and not talk while he walked around demanding things that people at the Embassy generally ignored. As a woman, I wanted to go up to the girl and say, "Hey, I understand why you are probably with this guy, but once you are in the States, you can get a divorce. You don't have to put up with that."

I didn't because it wasn't any of my business. She would probably figure it out once she got to the States. There were several, of what I thought looked like, mail order brides in the room that day, but who was I to judge? I was bringing home a "foreigner", too.

We hopped on an airplane as soon as we could and headed to Wisconsin. On the airplane, I quizzed my husband on family names and relationships. I had a big family, so he needed to be on top of that. My whole family met us and had a party to celebrate our arrival. We jumped right into life in Wisconsin. My husband got a job as a bartender at the local bar while finishing up his degree at the local University. My little hometown never knew what hit them. Can you imagine? Local patrons would belly up to the local watering hole, and there behind the bar was this guy with an accent, from a place that they had never heard of, asking them why they would ever mix orange juice and vodka (in Ukraine, you never mix vodka with anything, it's not the manly thing to do). I'll let you imagine what people thought of my husband, or maybe that is the subject of another book.

Robert Frost (1874-1963) wrote in his poem, *The Road Not Taken*, "Two roads diverged in a wood, and I- I took the one less traveled by, And that has made all the difference."

When I look back on my time in the Peace Corps, this line is the most applicable. Yes, I could have stayed in my hometown and continued living the life everyone around me had. Or I could take the path that no one I knew had taken. Not only had the path I had gone down changed me as a person and the way I saw the world, but it also changed the way people saw me. The people I had known for years were shocked to hear that I had done something as crazy as leaving Wisconsin. New people I meet to this day are also shocked to learn of my misadventures. I will always have a piece of that small-town girl in me, just as the constant desire to go out and see the world will always be a part of me, too.

When I returned home and people found out I had been in the Peace Corps, they often asked often asked, "So how was it?". What an impossible question to answer. How could I possibly whittle down two years of experiences into a single all-encompassing sentence? Heck, it took me a whole book to get some of my stories down on paper, or electronic tablet, as the case may be. A better, more accurate description of my experience as a Peace Corps Volunteer is best summed up by the singer/songwriter Jimmy Buffet and his immortal words in the song, *Changes in Latitudes, Changes in Attitudes* - "If we couldn't laugh, we would all go insane."

Most of us have THAT story, and some of us have many stories. How boring travel and life would be without those crazy moments. The stories that are so unbelievable that if you let it, will drive you crazy. Getting your butt slapped by some drunk guy as you walked down the street. Being told not to sit on cement, such as a front stoop, because it will freeze your ovaries and you won't have children. Having an old lady yell at you for pushing the hood of your coat off your head for a minute, because as we all know not having something on your head will give you pneumonia and you will die. All those things were nuggets of wisdom I picked up along the road and added to my life. Those travel mishaps are all part of the experience. If you have never been taken off of a train by armed international border guards, how boring of a trip that must have been. I have long since thought that those travel problems and hiccups are what makes a trip memorable.

For those of you reading this hoping for advice on whether to travel or take that giant step of moving away from your life and starting something new, it's not hard to see which side I am on. I can't promise that you are going to have the adventure that I did. I can only say that I wouldn't trade my two years with the Peace Corps for anything. Sure, things were frustrating, uncomfortable, and depressing, but I have also never laughed so hard with some amazing people that became lifelong friends. I was lucky to live somewhere that is completely different from what I knew, and because of that, developed a new perspective and understanding. Best of all, I found my partner in love and travel. What more could I or anyone ask for?

The road less traveled had brought me, with my new husband, back to Wisconsin. It was kind of a role reversal. Now, he was the one to try and figure out how to fit in and live in a place that was completely different than what he had left behind in Ukraine. As for me, the road less traveled may have led back home, but it would only be temporary. I was different, and it had made all the difference.

Kathy Ivchenko is the author of 'Awkward Stumbles and Fuzzy Memories: Memoir of a Peace Corps Volunteer', a memoir that is 25 years in the making, detailing her personal journey with the Peace Corps. With a Bachelor's Degree in Elementary Education from the University of Wisconsin-Whitewater and a Master's in Higher Education Administration from George Mason University, Ivchenko draws on her unique life experiences and lessons in her writing.

Ivchenko served in the Peace Corps Ukraine from 1994-1996, and again with her husband from 2000-2001, which has inspired her life-long love of travel. Her writing is packed with honesty and humor, and is often centered around travel and self-discovery